Baedeker St Paul, Mn, 55102

Venice

Contents

The Principal Places of Tourist Interest at a Glance

Preface

This Pocket Guide to Venice is one of the new generation of Baedeker city guides.

Baedeker pocket guides, illustrated throughout in colour, are designed to meet the needs of the modern traveller. They are quick and easy to consult, with the principal sights described in alphabetical order and practical details about opening times, how to get there, etc., shown in the margin.

Each guide is divided into three parts. The first part gives a general account of the city, its history, population, culture and so on; in the second part the principal sights are described; and the third part contains a variety of practical information designed to help visitors to find their way about and make the most of their stay.

The new guides are abundantly illustrated and contain numbers of newly drawn plans. At the back of the book is a large city map, and each entry in the main part of the guide gives the co-ordinates of the square on the map in which the particular feature can be located. Users of this guide, therefore, will have no difficulty in finding what they want to see.

How to use this book

Following the tradition established by Karl Baedeker in 1844, sights of particular interest, outstanding buildings, works of art, etc., as well as good hotels and restaurants are distinguished by either one ★ or two ★★ stars.

To make it easier to locate the various sights listed in the "A to Z" section of the Guide, their co-ordinates on the large city map are shown in red at the head of each entry.

Only a selection of hotels, restaurants and shops can be given: no reflection is implied, therefore, on establishments not included.

The symbol ⓘ on a town plan indicates the local tourist office from which further information can be obtained. The post-horn symbol indicates a post office.

In a time of rapid change it is difficult to ensure that all the information given is entirely accurate and up to date, and the possibility of error can never be completely eliminated. Although the publishers can accept no responsibility for inaccuracies and omissions, they are always grateful for corrections and suggestions for improvement.

Facts and Figures

Arms of the
City of Venice

General

Venice, in Italian Venezia, is the capital of the Veneto region, one of the 20 regions of the Republic of Italy. Officially entitled "Venezia Città", the city is situated in the north-eastern part of Italy on longitude 12°2' east and latitude 41°25' north.

Situation

The present commune of Greater Venice includes Marghera and Mestre on the mainland, the islands of Torcello, Burano and Murano, the part of the city on the Lido and Venice proper, i.e. the historical island city in the middle of the lagoon. In size Greater Venice covers 286sq.km/110sq.miles (161sq.km/62sq.miles of water, 125sq.km/ 48sq.miles of land) and the main island is 4.26km/2½ miles long and from 2.79km/1¾ miles wide at its broadest point to 1.33km/¾ mile at its narrowest. The circumference of the city, including the islands of San Giorgio and Giudecca, amounts to 13.7km/8½ miles. Of Greater Venice's 312,000 population 76,000 live in Venice proper (as compared with 200,000 in its heyday), 45,000 on islands and 191,000 on the mainland.

Area and population

For centuries the city in the lagoon has been divided into six districts or "sestieri": San Marco, Castello, Cannaregio, Santa Croce, San Polo and Dorsoduro, which includes Giudecca and San Giorgio.

Districts

Nowadays Greater Venice, like every Italian city, is governed by a Sindaco (Mayor) and Giunta Municipale (Municipal Council). Local government elections are held every five years.

Administration

Venice – city of the lagoon

Venice lies in the Laguna Veneta, a salt-water lagoon 40km/25 miles long and up to 15km/9¼ miles wide. This lagoon was formed in

Laguna Veneta

◀ *Multi-faceted Venice*

prehistoric times by silt deposits that built up an almost unbroken line of spits ("lidi", sing. Lido) about 20km/12½ miles out to sea from the flat Adriatic coastline. A breach in the spit was called a "porto" (pl. "porti").

Further deposits of mud formed islands within the lagoon and the original settlements on these islands gradually grew together to form Venice.

The city remained cut off as an island until 1846 when the causeway was built to the mainland to carry the railway line.

Piling

Venice consists of 118 flat islets, packed close together, and originally considered unsuitable for buildings because of their soft mud covering. The settlers then discovered that there was a solid layer of heavy clay beneath the mud and that buildings could be erected on piles driven down into this substratum. A horizontal layer of piling was then placed on top of the vertical piles, thus providing the foundations for almost all of Venice's 20,000 or so buildings.

Venice in Peril

Venice and its lagoon are in peril. Although there has been a water main from the mainland since 1884 (until then water was drawn from cisterns supplied by wells in the town) industrial effluent from Mestre and Porta Marghera is rotting the piles on which the city is built, and air pollution is eating away the stone walls of the buildings. Formerly the city was sinking at a rate of 200mm in each century, but since the mid-30s the subsidence has been increasing annually by 4–6mm. The land near the coast and the embankment are sinking at the rate of 2–3mm a year. From 1930 pumping of ground water to provide supplies for the Porto Marghera area had led to subsidence in the lagoon which was not halted until the construction of a water main in 1970. The extraction of methane in southern Polesine also led to subsidence of the bed of the lagoon until 1961 when production was moved further

View of Canal Grande and Santa Maria della Salute

to the south. The high tides (acqua alta) which occur between September and March have recently been getting higher, and between 1970 and 1986 they exceeded the 1.1m mark on 54 occasions. Since the dredging of the Lido approaches, and the construction of a ship canal between Mallamocco and Marghera, changes in the times of high water and the characteristics of the currents have been detected. An increase in the strength of the current and in the salt content of the water have had considerable adverse effects on the brickwork of Venetian buildings. Other reasons for deterioration in buildings are the aggressive effect of chemical waste (including nitrogen and phosphate compounds) in the lagoon, which has led to problems caused by the growth of algae in the canals; the harmful emissions in the atmosphere; the deterioration of wooden piles in the foundations of buildings in the city caused by micro-organisms; the growth of mould in the old, permanently damp buildings; and finally the droppings of Venice's innumerable pigeons. International organisations are trying to save the city. Almost every European country, plus the USA and Australia, has assumed sponsorship of particularly important buildings. Since the disastrous flooding of 1966 there have been innumerable conferences to look at ways of saving the city from "drowning". In 1985 it was finally decided to embark on the ten-year MOSE project (MOSE=modolo sperimentale elettromechanico). About 80 dykes and barriers consisting of tank-like cylinders have been constructed at three entrances to the lagoon, and these can be raised or lowered depending on the water level. It remains to be seen whether these measures will protect Venice from exceptionally high tides without endangering the essential ebb and flow of water in the canals.

Population and Religion

About 76,000 people still live in historic Venice, while a further 260,000 or so live in the neighbouring industrial districts of Mestre and Marghera whose refineries and dockyards attract a workforce from throughout Italy. Only about 2,000 people still commute daily from Venice proper to work in the industrial zones, as compared with 10 times that number who commute from the mainland every day to work in the island city.

Population

The Venetians are 99% Roman Catholic. Their Cardinal Archbiship bears the title of Patriarch. Pope John XXIII was Patriarch of Venice before his election to the Papacy.

Religion

Transport

The new economy of Venice is centred on the port of Marghera. Dating primarily from after the First World War, with its annual turnover of 24 million tons of goods this has become 24km/15 miles of quayside and container port, Italy's second largest industrial port.

Port

As an oil terminal, however, Marghera can hardly compete with Trieste which is able to accommodate supertankers. Although the channel through the lagoon has been dredged, there are no discharge facilities for oil-tankers of a tonnage greater than 80,000–90,000 because of the relatively shallow waters in this part of the Mediterranean.

The port for passenger ships is in the Canale di San Marco, diagonally opposite the Doge's Palace (see Palazzo Ducale). There are connections with all the main Adriatic ports as well as with Rhodes and Piraeus in Greece; Venice is also popular as the point of embarkation

Passenger shipping

for cruises which usually leave from Zattere and the Riva degli Schiavoni.

Airport

Marco Polo, Venice's international airport (Aeroporto Internazionale), is near Tessera, about 13km/8 miles north-east of Venice.

Railway

Since 1846 a railway bridge has linked the Santa Lucia railway terminal on the island of Venice with the mainland and the rest of the international rail network; Venice is served by direct express trains from virtually all the main European destinations.

Exit roads

Since 1933 Venice has also been joined to the mainland by a 3.6km/2¼ mile road bridge linking it with the Italian road system and, via the Milan–Trieste motorway, the European motorway network.

Car limits

Cars cannot be taken beyond the Tronchetto car park or the multistorey car park at the Piazzale Roma at the end of the road bridge. Beyond that point all movement in the city is either by boat or on foot.

Boats

Since the 118 islands which go to make up Venice are crammed very close together and are built on up to the very edges, while the waterways between the individual islands have been kept open, Venice has a network of 177 canals, most of them narrow, which act as the streets of the city. Nowadays the main means of transport is by the various types of motor boat, but the traditional barges and gondolas, operated by only one person, are still very much in evidence as are the troghetti (gondola ferries) which are craft rowed by more than one person.

Craft which operate a regular passenger service can be found on the Canal Grande and its continuation to the eastern tip of the city, as well as from the Riva degli Schiavoni and from Zattere to San Giorgio and Giudecca.

For journeys over a longer distance there are only two embarkation points, the Riva degli Schiavoni (for the Lido, Chioggia, Punta Sabbioni) and Fondamente Nuove (for Murano, Burano and Torcello). All other journeys have to be made on foot, unless you wish to hire a gondola or motor boat to serve as a taxi.

Gondolas

The gondolas are Venice's oldest form of boat. First mentioned in 697, they have since served mainly to carry passengers, but their number has shrunk from 10,000 in the 16th c. to only 400 today. It was decreed in 1562 that all gondolas must henceforth be painted black since the noble houses were overloading their craft with ornamentation. Every gondola is 10.15m/33¼ft long and 1.40m/4½ft wide and for reasons of distribution of weight the right-hand side is nine inches broader than the left. The gondolier stands at the stern. Eight different types of wood are used in a gondola and it weighs 700kg/1543lb.

Canal Grande

The embodiment of the glory of Venice is the Canal Grande, the Grand Canal, which winds like an inverted S through the city, dividing it into two halves. It is one of the tributaries of the River Brenta which flows through the lagoon at this point out into the sea. The knolls on the banks of this tributary projecting above the waters of the lagoon formed the island on which Venice stands, hence the time-honoured name of "Rivus Altus" (high bank) or, in its present form, Rialto.

With its length of 3.8km/2½ miles and its width of from 40 to 70m/130 to 230ft the Canal Grande is the largest of Venice's canals and with its magnificent palaces on either side has become one of the world's most famous "high streets".

Streets, squares, bridges

Besides its canals Venice also has 3000 streets. Apart from the general term "calle" these are also called "fondamenta" or "riva" (formerly embankment), "salizzada" (main street), "rugo" or "rugetta" (alley),

Gondolas – for centuries Venice's prime means of transport

"ramo" (cul de sac), "lista" (formerly the site of foreign embassies) and, finally, "rio terrà" (filled-in canal). There is only one "piazza", namely the Square of St Mark, and the smaller adjoining squares are called "piazzetta" (in front of the Doges' Palace, see Palazzo Ducale, and the Piazzetta dei Leoncini, near the Basilica of San Marco, see entry). All Venice's other squares are called "campo" or, if they are very small, "campiello".

The streets and alleys cross the canals by means of more than 400 bridges, three of them over the Canal Grande: the wooden Ponte dell'Accademia, the famous Ponte di Rialto (see entries) and the modern Ponte Scalzo near the station.

Culture

Its famous buildings, art treasures and many academic establishments make Venice one of Italy's great centres of culture. It has a university, founded in 1868 for industry and commerce, colleges for architecture, music and foreign languages, an Academy of Sciences, an Art Academy, a nautical and oceanographic institute and other higher education establishments and technical colleges. The Library of San Marco (1.2 million volumes) and the National Archive make their impact felt far beyond the confines of the city. As for museums, special mention should be made of the Museo Civico Correr, the Museo del Settecento Veneziano, the Archaeological Museum, the Museo d'Arte Moderna, the Galleria dell'Accademia, the Querini-Stampalia Picture Gallery, the Galleria Franchetti (see Ca' d'Oro), the Galleria Peggy Guggenheim (see Ca' Venier), the Museo Storico Navale and the Museo dell'Arte Vetraria (see Murano, glass museum).

In the 15th to 17th c. Venice became a renowned centre of art. Here – as in Florence and Rome – architecture, with Sansovino (see Prominent   Art

11

Querini-Stampalia Picture Gallery

La Fenice Theatre

Figures in Venetian History) and Palladio, but above all fine art, were the hallmarks of a whole epoch of European art, the Renaissance. The Venetian School of Painting, among the most important of all, began early in the 15th c. on Murano with Antonio and Barolomeo Vivarini and went on to produce such famous artists as Carpaccio, Bellini, Titian, Tintoretto and Veronese (see Prominent Figures in Venetian History). The fame of Venetian painting underwent a resurgence in the Rococo period with Tiepolo, Canaletto and Guardi (see Famous People). In the field of music Venice played a leading role with such innovators as Vivaldi and Monteverdi and in literature with Goldoni, a dramatist with a European reputation (see Famous People). Since the 19th c., when Venice capitulated to Napoleon, the city has failed to produce its own native-born artists but it has been the temporary home, particularly in the Romantic Period, of many internationally famed poets (Lord Byron, D'Annunzio) as well as such theatrical personalities as Eleanora Duse. Now Venice is again seeking to become a cultural centre. It hosts the "Biennale d'Arte" (modern art exhibition) every two years and has an annual film festival, an international festival of contemporary music and opera seasons in La Fenice, as well as prestige performances in its theatres and a host of other different productions staged in its two open-air theatres.

Commerce and Industry

Economic centre

Venice's main industries are tourism, glassmaking, chemicals, metallurgy, engineering and shipbuilding, and after centuries of economic decline the city is again becoming a centre for industry and commerce, especially in its mainland suburbs of Mestra and Marghera where besides plant for processing cotton and agricultural products there are enormous refineries and dockyards as well as a viable metallurgy sector. Since the 1920s, when it was founded on a mainland area liable

Old Customs House

to flooding and protected by dykes, this zone has grown to be a hive of industry and, as was intended, has come to provide jobs for the people of Venice.

The island of Murano is the centre of the glass industry. The famous Murano glass is exported throughout the world, as well as proving a great tourist attraction. There are 300 glassworks, employing about 4000 glassmakers. The people of the island of Burano have been makers of embroidered lace for generations, while throughout Venice there are many skilled artisans producing jewellery, textiles, and other handicrafts.

Glassmaking and other crafts

Tourism is the main industry of historic Venice (Venezia Città), with its 200 hotels, providing over half the working population with employment. Venice is also an administrative centre and home to the head offices of several banks and insurance companies. Consequently 80% of the population of the old city have jobs in the service sector.

Tourism and the service sector

Government of the Venetian City State under the Doges

Venice's situation between East and West and the political risks this engendered made it imperative to have a Constitution embodying checks and balances on political control. Venice was still a Republic which was represented by the Doge, underpinned by the aristocracy and ruled by two forces – the mutual interests of the patrician families, and their fundamental and mutual mistrust of one another, of the Doge and of the people. The sole aim of the constitution was to neutralise any individual build-up of power and to ensure the two forces were evenly balanced.

Consitution

The people and the Church were soon eliminated from the political process; the power of the Doges was increasingly curbed. After 1229 the Doge of Venice had to swear to a "Promissio", to sign an agreement in which the electors stipulated the terms for the future government.

The Great Council, the Consiglio Maggiore, was the real political power. Its members were the "Nobili", the aristocracy, whose interests, identical with the interests of the State, lay in trade, which must be pushed, promoted and protected.

It was not until late in the 16th and 17th c. when, with the discovery of new routes, trade took a different direction and Venice slowly declined in importance, that the interests of the nobility and the State were no longer identical.

If trade went well then all was well with the city and with it the people and the polity. Individually the diverse interests which made up the State would have been incapable of embarking on the more risky ventures or of carrying out the more ambitious projects; collectively they had the strength, the power and the tenacity.

Office of Doge

The Head of State of the Republic of Venice was the Doge, whose seat was his palace (see A to Z, Palazzo Ducale). Pauluccio Anafesto, the first Doge (Latin "dux"=Italian Doge cf. English Duke), assumed office in A.D. 697; Manin, the last Doge, handed back the Doge's cap in 1797 with the words "it will not be needed any more". Over those 1100 years the Republic of Venice had been represented by 120 Doges. Their badge of office, the Doge's cap, was based on the Phrygian fisherman's hat, rising to a point on a stiffened base and set with gold and jewels to the value of 194,000 ducats.

Originally "primus inter pares" (first among equals) the Doge was elected and endorsed by the populace: "this is your Doge if he pleases you". His power was virtually limitless: he negotiated in his own right with Emperors and Popes, decided on war or peace, personally sought out his officials, his officers, his successor, often his co-Regents. His councillors ("pregadi") had an advisory function only. He exercised jurisdiction and possessed the right of pardon.

G. Bellini: Doge Giovanni Mocenigo　　*L. Bastiani: Doge Francesco Foscari*

Venetian Lion on the Doges Palace

When in the 10th c. Doge Pietro Candiano IV (959–976) attempted to make the office of Doge hereditary and thus to alter the constitution to rule by a family there was a revolt in 976. The Doge's palace and the Basilica went up in flames and the Doge and his young son perished in San Marco.

This event prompted ever more rigorous curbs on the power of the Doge: the law that the Doge could no longer appoint his co-Regents was followed by the law that the Doge could no longer appoint his successor (mid 11th c.). The Small Council (Consiglio Minore) was formed to watch over the head of state. Finally the populace lost its voice in the election of the Doge – now it was "this is your Doge" (mid 12th c.) – and was replaced by the Great Council (Consiglio Maggiore).

As with the Pope, election took the form of a conclave. The balloting procedure was extremely complicated. Thirty members of the Great Council would be balloted for, and then the ballot would be for 9 of them. They nominated 40 provisional electors who in turn elected 12 by lot who then elected 25. These were reduced to 9 who then each nominated 5. These 45 were reduced by casting lots to 11; it needed 9 of the 11 votes to choose the final 41 who would elect the Doge.

Election

The future Doge must amass at least 25 of these votes. He was elected for life. This system of election offered every noble the chance to take part without allowing any group or family to exercise undue influence and thus impair the basic principles of the Constitution.

In terms of political duties the office of the Doge, from the 13th c. onwards, was more or less the equivalent of a modern State President; he represented the State at home and abroad, had a seat on every body in the Government (but only one vote), presided over the Great Council, had to bring about decisions and control the officers of the State.

Functions

The list of duties he could not undertake was, however, entirely geared to the specific interests of the Republic and its Constitution, which, as such, was unique in the world. A catalogue of those duties not open to him was drawn up in 1600; the Doge was not allowed to appoint his own men nor could he hold any external office (this affected Doge Enrico Dandolo, conqueror of Byzantium, who was not allowed to accept the Crown of Austria). No member of the Doge's family was allowed to take part in a business venture; sons and daughters could not marry outside the Republic without the permission of the Great Council. In the Promissio (see Constitution) the Doge must swear not to undertake any coup, not to seek to restore the former powers of the office, not to open any letters from outside Powers in the absence of the Councils nor to write any, not to receive envoys, not to accept presents (other than flowers, herbs or rosewater). His Councillors (pregadi) were appointed by the Great Council. He was no longer allowed to erect or improve public buildings, or to have any possessions other than those connected with his office of Doge.

Finally in the 16th and 17th c. came still further restrictions; even in his private apartments he was forbidden to receive foreign envoys or generals. His sons were not permitted to go out of the State; his Consort was no longer to be crowned and no longer had an official retinue. Similarly he and his family were forbidden to maintain relations with outside sovereigns. Although in the early years of the office the Doge still was at the head of the army, after the 14th c. the duty was hardly exercised. If he should appear on the battlefield it was to embolden his people, not to lead them. There was one exception: Francesco Morosini, the Doge elected in 1688, who had won back the Peloponnese in 1686/87 for 30 years (in the course of the fighting a Venetian shell blew up the Parthenon on the Acropolis in Athens) and who continued to command the Venetian fleet until 1690.

Great Council

After 1172 the Great Council, which drew together the great noble families of the Republic, became the supreme legislative body of the State and watched over the Doge. In the early 13th c. the Great Council had 35 members. When this number had risen steeply the Council enacted a "serrata" in 1297 decreeing that henceforth no-one whose family was not recorded in the "Libro d'Oro", the register of the aristocracy of the Republic, could become a member of the Council (when the Republic ended there were 1218 names in this Golden Book).

The Great Council was only directly consulted on absolutely basic matters and confined itself otherwise to the acceptance of statements of accounts but its members did determine the membership of the difference bodies charged with executing the affairs of State, and it elected the Doge from its own ranks. Each noble held an office in the State organisation, usually as an unpaid servant of the State. He was not allowed to refuse any duty he was called upon to discharge or decline any command. Anyone who failed when in office, whether or not it was his own fault, was subject to the harshest penalties.

Their compliance with the strict laws created by the members of the Great Council in the interests of the State was as unquestioning and unconditional as the obedience they required of the other members of the polity.

Silver Book

The middle-class families were recorded in the Silver Book. Although they took no part in the decision-making process, they were responsible for the administration of the State and putting Government decrees into effect. The families recorded in the Gold and Silver Books amounted to less than 15% of Venice's population but owned almost 90% of its capital assets.

**Senate
(Small Council)**

After 976 the Senate or "Small Council" gradually came to be the supervisory body for the Doges. It was not until 1229 that it became an official authority, with narrowly defined tasks and the title of "Consiglio dei Pregadi" (its members were requested, i.e. "pregadi" or prayed, by written invitation to attend the session). The Senate consisted of 60 members elected from the Great Council, the Doge and the "Zonta", which was made up of 6 patricians from the Great Council, 5 representatives of the provinces on the mainland and 5 representatives of the religious Orders. Other members of the circle were the closest of the Doge's advisers, the delegates from the Judiciary, the Council of Ten, the "Avvogadori" (constitutional judges), the "Cattaveri" (tax assessors) and the "Provveditori" (overseers).

The Senate was in effect the governing Parliament – answerable to the Great Council but entitled to take major decisions: it decided on peace or war, what decrees should be submitted to the Great Council and appointed all important State officials, office-holders, bishops and prelates. It also set up and supervised all the committees charged with aligning the administration to political and social developments.

The Collegio was the Cabinet of the Republic of St Mark. It was composed of the Doge and his six Councillors, the three Magistrates who presided over the Courts of Justice and the chairmen of the three groups in the Zonta. The Collegio prepared all the Bills to be submitted to the Senate, decided on what should be kept from the Senate on grounds of secrecy, received and heard foreign envoys and was responsible for the delicate negotiations with the Church of Rome. In addition it was the supreme court of appeal for the Judiciary. Also the Collegio acted on behalf of the Republic in dealing with representatives of Foreign Powers. Its members were elected from the Great Council and the Senate.

Collegio

The Council of Ten, the most sinister and most feared body in the Venetian Government, was meant to act as a liaison between the legislature, i.e. the Great Council and the Senate, and the executive, i.e. the Doge, and the Administration, such as the judiciary. It was called into being when in 1310 Baiamonte Tiepolo made a vain attempt to break the rule of the nobility, but did not emerge in its final form until the Decree of the Great Council in 1455.

Council of Ten

The Senate decided every year on the 10 members of this Council. The Doge and his six councillors also sat in on the Council of Ten, together with a constitutional lawyer (Avvocador) whose job it was to ensure that the decisions of the Council of Ten accorded with the laws and the constitution. The names of the members of the Council of Ten were kept secret.

The multifarious tasks and duties of the Council of Ten can be summed up as guarding State security. They were mainly concerned with dealing with matters of planned, attempted or accomplished high treason, espionage, sabotage, conspiracy, etc. The Council was also responsible for keeping watch on the morals of the city, and preventing and punishing suspected duels (which were strictly forbidden), violent acts and anything that amounted to a disturbance of the peace. And finally the Council was charged with prosecuting acts endangering trade and assuming the responsibility for getting the greatest possible yields from the State enterprises such as the glass industry or mining and forestry on the mainland.

The Council of Ten was the absolute organ of public safety with virtually unlimited powers. It was a watchdog over the most intimate life of the citizen and against its verdict there was no appeal, even in the event of summary judgements meted out without preamble. Any Venetian could be summoned before the Council, even the Doge, and Marin Falier, the Doge executed in 1355 for alleged high treason, was only one among many. It was also up to the Council of Ten, after the death of a Doge, to judge how he had fulfilled his office and those who were left behind had to bear the brunt of the praise, censure or even damages arising from any blunders.

For these extremely onerous official duties the Council of Ten had three invaluable aids at its disposal:

(1) an efficient and unobtrusive secret police, which could do its bidding in any corner of the world;

(2) the "lion's mouths", the letterboxes for secret denunciations. Any Venetian who noticed anything suspicious could turn this into a denunciation by writing it down and posting his communication in a "lion's mouth". He had to sign it, together with two witnesses (a necessary measure to prevent malicious or defamatory denunciations), but the person denounced would never know who it was had denounced him;

(3) the merchant traders. The merchants of Venice, travelling on every sea and in almost every part of the civilised world, were always on the spot for gathering the very best information about trade and politics – in the markets and the bazaars, and in the Courts of the powerful. And every returning Venetian merchant not only brought back with him a ship full of wares but also proved a mine of information for the secret service.

ᶜor centuries the Government of the Venetian Republic was the best-informed Government in the world – further grounds for the city's rise to power.

The Council of Ten could count upon these three aids and usually knew exactly what it was about! As a rule everything happened very swiftly; suddenly the secret police would appear, arrest the suspect and whisk him away to appear before the Council. The accusation would be read out and if it could not be conclusively refuted the accused would immediately be found guilty. If the miserable wretch still did not confess, this would be followed by the torture – and then the sentence which could be a flogging, the loss of a hand, gouging out the eyes, etc. but in about half the cases the sentence was death. The famous executions between the Colonne di Marco e Teodoro (see entry) on the Molo were relatively rare. More often than not the condemned were discreetly throttled in their cells or taken out to sea at night and drowned in the lagoon between San Giorgio and the Lido.

Anyone condemned "in absentia" was also as good as dead, even if he thought himself safely abroad. The Council of Ten had its secret police, and the police had their "Venetian dagger", a razor-sharp blade of glass, sheathed in metal, as broad as a man's thumb, which, when plunged into the victim's body up to the hilt, would immediately snap off at the haft. The victim's skin would straightaway close up over the wound, leaving what appeared to be only a slight graze at the point of entry. It was some considerable time before the rest of the world caught up with this particular Venetian secret weapon.

The fact that the Council of Ten also supervised the preparations for important State ceremonies and receptions and even had a hand, in the background, in their organisation, shows how wide was the range of their duties.

Three Chief Magistrates (Inquisitori)

The "Chiefs" jointly conducted examinations and brought them to the Council of Ten for their decision. They consisted of two members of the Ten and one of the Doge's Councillors. If they felt a communication was too dangerous it was not shown to the Council of Ten or the Doge but lodged in the form of a sealed document.

Three Avvogadori

Although termed simply "advocates" these lawyers in fact acted as judges of the Constitution and public prosecutors. It was their job to ensure that decisions in the Great Council, the Senate and the Council of Ten accorded with the laws and if necessary they could exercise their veto. They also watched over the observance of treaties, the collection of fines and the correctness of commercial and private legal procedures.

The institution of the "Avvogadori", which had existed since the 12th c., was, therefore, a precursor of the independent administration of justice that exists today in all democratic States. In this sense it should be considered in conjunction with the "Quarantia".

This institution, consisting of 40 (i.e. "quaranta") members, had existed since 1179. Originally merely a court of appeal of no more than 40 patricians, it rapidly developed into the actual judicial body of the Republic. In the 14th c. its workload was so great that the "Quarantia" had to be split into two, becoming the Quarantia Civil, the court dealing with civil cases, and Quarantia Criminal, responsible for non-political criminal cases such as murder, robbery, etc. Two hundred years later the civil complaints, such as defamation and fraud, had become so numerous that the Quarantia Civil had to be further subdivided into the Quarantia Civil Vecchia and the Quarantia Civil Nuova.

Quarantia

All these State organs gradually created a nework of honorary or paid officials and institutions that painstakingly performed the duties they were charged with.

Provveditori, Cattaveri, Censori

Chief among these were the Provveditori, the overseers, nobles who superintended and directed indispensable organisations and projects. Hence the "Provveditori de Mar", a body responsible for fitting out the war fleet, recruiting seamen and rowers, etc., or Provveditori who looked after the welfare institutions or were concerned with the churches, monasteries and religious associations.

Less obtrusive but much less pleasant were the Cattaveri, the tax assessors. Every Venetian, regardless of rank and person, had to allow them to inspect absolutely everything he possessed and then let the assessor dictate to him how much – and it was always a considerable sum – he had to pay the State in taxes. And woe betide anyone making a false declaration: they would soon find themselves arraigned in front of the Council of Ten.

Last but by no means least there were the "Censori". Drawn from the Great Council, their sole task was to prevent cheating in the elections for the various bodies and offices. It is said – and this speaks for the honour of the Republic of St Mark – that throughout all those centuries their services were hardly ever called upon.

Famous People

Canaletto
(Giovanni Antonio
Canal)
1697–1768

Canaletto was one of the last of the great Venetian artists. Born in Venice, he started painting in the theatre then studied in Rome and turned to nature studies. His first great success in Venice was with "vedute" (views) then after a second stay in Rome in 1742 he started painting imaginary landscapes before finally taking up the genre which he made all his own of finely detailed townscapes alive with carnivals, festivals and processions.

Canaletto spent two periods in England (1746–50 and 1751–53) and it is there that most of his works can be found. In Venice a "capriccio" by Canaletto is to be seen in the Accademia di Belle Arte.

Giacomo
Casanova
1725–98

His fame as a lover and his elegant philandering have made Giacomo Casanova a legendary son of Venice. His invented title of "Chevalier de Seingalt" point to his being by nature an adventurer. He made a spectacular escape from the Venetian State Prison by a peculiarly hazardous route. On his travels throughout Europe (in various posts) he broke many a maidenly heart. Constantly embroiled in disputes and frequently on the run, Casanova finally found a post in 1785 as Librarian to Count Waldstein in Bohemia where he wrote his "Memoirs" (in French), an important record of the society of his day. He also penned a Utopian novel and other historical, mathematical and scientific works.

Enrico Dandolo
c. **1110–1205**

Dandolo, scion of an old-established noble Venetian family, was 82 before he was elected Doge. Despite his age he never shrank from any military confrontation that might secure and advance Venetian influence in the Eastern Mediterranean and thus he drove the Pisans out of Istria. As a greybeard of 94 and totally blind, with the lords of the Fourth Crusade, he helped conquer the Byzantine Empire of the Eastern Church. On the fall of Constantinople and Dalmatia he secured for Venice a great share of the treasures captured as booty, built staging-posts on the route to Constantinople and finally made Venice into a World Power. He died in 1205 in Constantinople.

Francesco Foscari
c. **1373–1457**

Francesco Foscari, elected Doge in 1423, continued the Venetian policy of expansion; after 1426 he conducted the four Milanese wars with the other Northern Italian city states and secured for the city its greatest territorial expansion – from Brescia to Ravenna. In 1454 the Peace of Lodi ended the centuries of fighting for sovereignty in Northern Italy. During this time, however, Foscari neglected policy in the East so in 1454 he finally had to sign a treaty with the Sultan abandoning Venice's supremacy in the Eastern Mediterranean.

In 1407 Foscari was deposed, thanks to the opposition of the Lorendano family, and his son Jacopo was banished. His fate and that of his oft-banished son inspired poets (Lord Byron) and composers (Verdi).

Carlo Goldoni
1707–93

The only great poetic writer in the history of that city of commerce, Venice, Goldoni introduced realism into Italian comedy, superseding the commedia dell'arte with comedies of manners that had much in common with Molière. He wrote as many as 136 comedies, including "The Servant of Two Masters" and "La Locandiera".

After studying law and philosophy Goldoni worked from 1744 to 1748 as a lawyer in Pisa, but his youthful involvement with the theatre led him on his return to Venice to begin writing plays from 1748 to 1753 for the Teatro di Sant'Angelo and then, until 1762, for the Teatro di San Luca.

Giacomo Casanova

Carlo Goldoni

Claudio Monteverdi

In 1762 the competition from rival playwrights caused Goldoni to leave for Paris where he was the Director of the Italian Theatre until 1764 and also mounted productions of his own plays. Impoverished by the Revolution, he died in 1793.

The impact of Claudio Monteverdi on music continued into the 18th c. Born in Cremona, Monteverdi was originally a scholar of composition in his home town (until 1590) and then a musician and Choirmaster at the Court of Mantua (until 1612). From 1613 until his death he worked as the Choirmaster of San Marco in Venice.

Claudio Monteverdi 1567–1643

Moving away from the rigid musical forms of the 16th c. Monteverdi developed greater freedom in styles of music but what made him the first great opera-composer with his "Orfeo", "Ulisse" and "Poppea", and whose influence was to be felt by such contrasting composers as Gluck and Richard Wagner, was his innovatory power of conceiving the drama as a whole in terms of music.

Marco Polo, whose travels changed the concept of the world of his time and focused the attention of Europeans on the distant East, was 17 when in 1271 his father and uncle took him with them from Venice on their journey to trade with China. After taking over three years crossing the continent of Asia they arrived at the Court of Kublai Khan, the Mongol Emperor. Marco Polo spent the next 17 years holding high office and travelling in the service of the Khan who finally in 1292 gave his permission for them to return to Europe. Marco Polo's account of his travels was dictated to his fellow captive Rusticiano during his sojourn in a Genoese gaol (1298–99). After his release he returned to Venice where he died in 1324.

Marco Polo 1254–1324

The Florentine Sansovino left his mark as no other architect could on the townscape of Venice when after 1527 he was appointed First Architect and Engineer of the Republic. He had a hand in or was responsible for the building of no less than 15 of the city's churches and public buildings including the Library of San Marco, the Mint (now the Biblioteca Marciana), the Logetta di San Marco, the Church of San Francesco della Vigna, the Palazzo Correr and the statues of Mars and Neptune in the courtyard of the Doge's Palace.

Sansovino (Jacopo Tatti) 1486–1570

He died in the city in 1570 at the age of 84.

Tintoretto, the son of a silk-dyer ("tintore"), not only holds a place in the annals of Venetian art as an indefatigable, inspired artist but also has a place in history for being an artist with a businesslike approach. Born in Venice, he left the city only once in his lifetime (he is known to have journeyed to Mantua in 1580) but was, nevertheless, influenced

Tintoretto (Jacopo Robusti) 1518–94

Famous People

Marco Polo

Tintoretto

Antonio Vivaldi

by the major artists of his time (e.g. Michelangelo) and the influence of Titian is apparent in the contrasting effects of light and shade in his paintings. The themes of his work tended to be taken from the Old and New Testaments.

His work in Venice can be found in the Galleria dell'Accademia ("The Miracle of St Mark", "Cain and Abel"), in the Church of San Giorgio Maggiore ("The Last Supper"), in San Marcuola ("The Last Supper"), in the Church of Santa Maria della Salute ("The Wedding at Cana"), in the Church of Santa Maria Mater Domini ("The Finding of the True Cross by St Helena"), in the Church of San Rocco ("The Healing of the Stricken") and, above all, in the Scuola di San Rocco (Christ before Pilate", "Christ Carrying the Cross", "Moses Striking Water from the Rock", "The Feeding of the Five Thousand").

Titian
(Tiziano Vecellio)
c. 1477–1576

In the middle of the 16th c. Titian, descendant of a family of artists, was the most sought-after painter in all Europe. He is thought to have come to Venice in 1508, where he was taught by Bellini and Giorgione and worked with them on their frescoes. He did not remain in the city, however, though he always maintained a household there; in 1511 he moved to the Court of Padua, after 1516 to Ferrara and from 1523 lived in Mantua. In 1533 he was elevated to the nobility and named as Court Painter. From 1543 he was a close friend of Pope Paul III. His most important patrons were the Emperor Charles V and his son Philip II of Spain. He died in Venice of the plague in 1576 at the age of 86 according to some historians, although others put his age at 91 or even 99.

In Venice his work can be seen in the Galleria dell'Accademia ("The Presentation of the Virgin", "St John the Baptist", "Pietà"), in the Chiesa dei Gesuiti ("Martyrdom of St Laurence"), in the Palazzo Ducale ("St Christophorus"), in the Church of Santa Maria dei Frari ("The Assumption of the Virgin", "Madonna of the Pesaro Family"), in the Church of San Salvatore ("The Annunciation") and in the Conti Collection ("St George").

Paolo Veronese
(Paolo Caliari)
1528–88

As his name implies, Veronese was born in Verona, but he nevertheless ranks with Tintoretto and Titian as one of the great artists of Venice in the Late Renaissance.

After working in 1552 on Mantua Cathedral, his home from 1554 was in Venice. Certain ambiguities in his "The Last Supper" actually brought him into conflict with the Inquisition but he made changes and characteristically retitled the painting "The Supper in the House of Levi". He was only able to complete all his commissions with the aid of a large studio and many assistants who transformed his drawings into paintings that reproduced his style.

His canvases are compositions on a grand scale that, with their gods and buffoons, monkeys, Moors and other exotic subjects, achieve a joyous splendour of sumptuous magnificence.

In Venice his works can be seen in the Church of San Sebastiano (ceiling and wall frescoes), in the Galleria dell'Accademia ("The Supper in the House of Levi") and in the Doges' Palace (ceiling and wall frescoes).

Not only was Vivaldi Venice's most important composer, he also, through his development of the solo concerto, made a substantial contribution to European music.

In 1703 Vivaldi entered the priesthood and from that time worked intermittently until 1740 as a violin teacher, conductor and composer in the Ospedale della Pietà in Venice. Ranked as one of the greatest violinists of his time, he was highly thought of by Johann Sebastian Bach who, without asking his permission (which was not so unusual at that time), transposed several of Vivaldi's own violin works for the organ, needless to say under his own name.

After centuries of neglect Vivaldi's work, of which some 770 pieces are known today, was rediscovered in 1926.

Antonio Vivaldi
1678–1741

History of Venice

About 1000 B.C.	An Illyrian people, the Veneti, successfully settle as farmers and traders in the Upper Adriatic.
190 B.C.	The Veneti are annexed into the Roman Empire; Padua becomes the wealthiest city in the Imperium Romanum after Rome.
A.D. 375	Beginning of the great migrations when the Huns sweep into Europe.
395	Division of the Empire by Theodosius into the Western Roman Empire (capital Ravenna) and the Eastern Roman Empire (capital Byzantium).
452	The Veneti are forced to flee from Attila and his Huns into the swampland of the lagoon.
476	Final destruction of the Western Roman Empire. Theodoric the Great founds an Ostrogothic Kingdom in Italy
553	End of the Gothic Kingdom; the troops of Justinian, the Eastern Roman Emperor, under their Commander Narses, occupy the lagoons. The cities of Venetia are placed under the Eastern Roman tribunes.
568	The Langobards take possession of all of Northern Italy. The Veneti finally settle on the islands in the lagoon. Their territory continues to belong to the Eastern Roman Empire.
697	Election of the first Doge (Latin "dux"=leader). He is Pauluccio-Anafesto who governs from the island of Heraclea.
742–755	During his rule Doge Teodato Ipato makes his seat the town of Malamocco on the Lido.
809	Charlemagne conquers the Lombard Kingdom. His son, Pepin, makes an-ineffectual attempt to capture the Venetian islands. The Venetians forsake Malamocco to retreat behind barricades on "Rivus Altus". The lagoon eventually stays in the Eastern Roman Empire and as a reward the Emperor in Constantinople grants the Venetians the status of a kind of Free State with an elected Doge at its head. Rivus Altus is built upon while the other island towns, Torcello and Malamocco, go into decline. The city is initially called "Civitas Venetiarum" and finally simply "Venetia".
810	With the Treaty of Aachen between Charlemagne and the Eastern Roman Emperor Michael I the Venetians obtain greater independence from Byzantium.
About 829	Venetian adventurers carry off the bones of the Apostle Mark from Alexandria to the Rialto, thus giving the Venetian State, which now calls itself the State of "San Marco", its own Patron Saint.
About 1000	Venice demands true independence from Constantinople, allies itself with the German Emperors, at that time Kings of Italy, and builds up its own empire. Venice conquers Istria and Dalmatia, sets up trading-posts throughout the Mediterranean and commands the greatest and most effective fleet in the Mediterranean.
1172	With the eventual introduction of the Great Council the constitution of the Republic is established, thus ensuring the hegemony of the nobility until the end of the Republic.

Venice as Italy's Third Power concludes peace with Emperor Barbarossa and Pope Alexander III who thus proclaim the lagoon city an equal partner. — 1177

Under the leadership of Doge Enrico Dandolo, blind and aged 92, Venice leads the ships of the Fourth Crusade which is persuaded to voyage to (Constantinople instead of the Holy Land and to conquer the Eastern Roman Empire. — 1202

After the conquest of Constantinople and the victory over Eastern Rome the Venetians keep for themselves three-eighths of the captured territory and Venice makes itself indispensable to the "Latin Empire" set up by the Crusaders in Constantinople.
Venice is the master of trade throughout the Eastern Mediterranean and a World Power. — 1204

Beginning of the war with Genoa, Venice's rival city state for supremacy in the Levantine trade. — 1210

After 170 years of fighting Venice finally achieves naval superiority over Genoa. It is now the absolute centre of world trade. — 1380

Venice expands on the mainland and conquers the territory of Lombardy almost as far as Milan. It calls its mainland possessions "Terra Firma". — 1389–1484

The city has a population of 200,000 and commands a fleet of over 45 galleys, 300 large and 3000 medium-sized trading vessels, with a total complement of almost 40,000 seamen. Venice is by far the richest city in the West. — 1423

The Turks conquer Constantinople and thus commences the slow decline of Venice as a World Power. — 1453

With the discovery of America by Columbus predominance in world trade gradually shifts from Venice to Lisbon, London, and the Low Countries. — 1492

The Papal States, led by Pope Julius II, unite with Spain, France and Germany against Venice in the League of Cambrai. The struggle weakens the city state. — 1508

End of the fighting with the League, leaving the city utterly exhausted, financially and politically, but managing to retain a good many of its conquests. — 1519

Venice once again controls the Peloponnese. The city is wealthy and a centre of banking. — 1684–1718

In the Treaty of Passarowitz Venice cedes most of its trading-posts in the Levant to the Ottoman Empire. — 1718

Napoleon I conquers the Republic of Saint Mark, without meeting any opposition. The city is separated from the surrounding territory. — 1797

The city belongs to the Napoleonic Kingdom of Italy. — 1805

Venice falls to Austria. — 1815

In an uprising the Venetians, led by Daniele Manin, succeed in obtaining 15 months of independence. The rebellion is put down by General Radetzky of Austria. — 1848–49

Canaletto: View of Venice at the Basin of St Marks (1745–50)

1866	Venice is incorporated into the new Kingdom of Italy.
1958	Giuseppe Roncalli, Patriarch of Venice, becomes Pope John XXIII.
1985	To protect Venice from high tides the 10-year MOSE project is agreed. About 80 dykes, consisting of huge tank-like cylinders which can be raised or lowered depending on the water-level, are constructed at three entrances to the lagoon.
1989	More than 200,000 visitors to the Pink Floyd concert on July 15th leave mountains of rubbish and cause damage to buildings in and around St Mark's Square.
1991	In April the Lion of St Mark's is restored to its position on the Molo (quayside).
1994	The crypt of St Mark's Basilica is reopened after restoration work.

Quotations

"Streets full of water. Please advise."
(Telegram on arriving in Venice)

Robert Benchley
20th c. Humorist

"Underneath Day's azure eyes
Ocean's nursling, Venice lies,
A peopled labyrinth of walls."

Shelley
19th c. poet

"Venice is like eating an entire box of chocolate liqueurs at one go."

Truman Capote
Author, 1961

"Once did she hold the gorgeous East in fee,
And was the safeguard of the West: the worth
Of Venice did not fall below her birth,
Venice, the eldest child of liberty.
She was a maiden city, bright and free;
No guile seduced, no force could violate;
And when she took unto herself a mate,
She must espouse the everlasting sea.
And what if she had seen those glories fade,
Those titles vanish, and that strength decay,
Yet shall some tribute of regret be paid
When her long life hath reached its final day:
Men are we, and must grieve when even the shade
Of that which once was great has passed away."

"The State is all; it is for the individual unconditionally to serve the State. No one person may rise above the others, no cult of personality will be tolerated."

Constitution
of the Republic

"Desposamus te mare, in signum veri perpetuique dominii"
(O sea, we wed thee as a sign of true and everlasting dominion)

Wedding
with the Sea

"It seems to me less difficult to have established this city on the face of the bottomless waters than to have united and led so many spirits in the same direction and despite the differing inclinations by which they are moved as individuals to have maintained the corporate body of this Republic, its power intact and unshaken."

Count Avaux
17th c.
ambassador

"Goods circulate around this splendid city like the streams of water that spring from the fountain."

Marino da Canala
1267

"The territory of Venetia is bordered in the South by the eminence of Ravenna and by the Po, in the East by the smiling cities of the Ionian coast. Here the tides suddenly retreat to reveal the changing face of the flooded land then flow back to cover it again. Your dwellings are built, like sea-birds' nests, half on sea and half on land, spread, as the Cyclades, over the surface of the waters. Through manmade earthworks you know how to bind your dwellings together. You heap up the sand to break the force of the raging waters and your walls, seemingly fragile, brave the force of the flood."

Cassiodorus
c. 490–580

"It is the finest highway to be found in the whole world, lined by the finest houses, and it passes through the whole of the city. The houses are very lofty and grand and of good stone and the older ones are painted over all, and they have stood there a hundred years. The others that have been built in the last century have façades of white marble

Philippe
de Commynes
Ambassador, 1495

Quotations

Albrecht Dürer

J. W. von Goethe

Thomas Mann

that comes from Istria and of porphyry. Inside they all have no less than two chambers with gilded panels, rich chimneypieces of hewn marble and beds with gilded posts and the other chambers are also gilded and painted and furnished very well within. It is the most triumphant street I have ever seen, it is the most joyous city I ever saw."

Albrecht Dürer
1471–1528

(On the subject of the painter Bellini following Dürer's stay in Venice) "Giambellini, he that had already praised me to diverse gentlemen, he was most desirous to have something of me and is himself come to me and begged me that I should make something for him, vouchsafing that he would make payment for it."

Goethe
1749–1832
"Italian Journey"

"It was written, then, on my page in the Book of Fate that at five in the afternoon of the twenty-eighth day of September in the year 1786, I should see Venice for the first time as I entered this beautiful island-city, this beaver-republic . . . I have found comfortable lodgings . . . not far from the Piazza San Marco. My windows look out on to a narrow canal between high houses; immediately below them is a single-span bridge, and opposite, a narrow crowded passage. This is where I shall live until my parcel for Germany is ready and I have had my fill of sightseeing, which may be some time."

Carlo Goldoni
18th c. Venetian

"They sing in the squares, on the streets and on the canals. The vendors sing as they cry their wares, the workers sing as they leave their workplaces, the gondoliers sing as they wait for custom."

Thomas Mann
20th c. writer
"Death in Venice"

"He saw it once more, that most astounding of landing-places, that breathtaking composition of fantastic buildings, which the Republic ranged to meet the awed gaze of the approaching seafarer; the airy splendour of the palace and the Bridge of Sighs, the columns of lion and saint on the shore, the glory of the projecting flank of the Basilica of St Mark, the vista of gateway and great clock. Looking, he thought that to come to Venice by the station is like entering a palace by the back door. No one should approach, save by the high seas as he was doing now, this most improbable of cities."

Emperor
Napoleon
1769–1821

(On St Mark's Square)
"The most beautiful drawing-room in Europe, for which it is only fitting that the heavens should serve as a ceiling."

Petrarch
Letters, 1364

"Venice is a city rich in gold, but richer still in beauty, mighty in its possessions, but mightier by its virtue; which is founded on solid marble but is yet more secure upon the foundations of the unswerving

28

unity of its population, and which, better than by the sea, is protected and safeguarded by the sagacity and the wisdom of its offspring."

"Venice is not only a special city, unlike any other in Italy, but it is also a special region, differing from any other region of Italy, with its own soil, its own sky, its own climate and its own air."

Hippolyte Taine
1828–93

"As I was returning home late one night on the gloomy canal, the moon appeared suddenly and illuminated the marvellous palaces and the tall figure of my gondolier towering above the stern of the gondola, slowly moving his huge sweep. At that moment he uttered a cry like a wild creature, a kind of deep groan that rose in crescendo to a prolonged "Oh!" and ended with the simple exclamation "Venezia!" This was followed by other sounds of which I have no distinct recollection, so much moved was I at the time. Such were the impressions that to me appeared the most characteristic of Venice during my stay there, and they remained with me until the completion of the second act of "Tristan", and possibly even suggested to me the prolonged tones of the shepherd's horn at the beginning of the third act."

Richard Wagner
Mein Leben, 1911

Venice from A to Z

Suggestions for sightseeing during a short visit to Venice will be found under the heading Sightseeing Programme in the Practical Information Section.

Note

Since opening times of museums and churches in Italy often change, it is unfortunately not always possible to give current details. To avoid disappointment it is advisable to enquire about possible changes before making a visit.

Accademia (Academy)

See Galleria dell'Accademia

Ala Napoleonica (Napoleonic Wing)   K 5

The west side of the Piazza di San Marco (see entry) is formed by the Ala Napoleonica which was built in 1810 by order of Napoleon I.

Location
Piazza di
San Marco

Quay
San Marco

The work was entrusted to the architect Giuseppe Soli who simply copied the two lower floors of the Procuratie Nuove (see entry), omitted the third floor in order not to spoil the proportions of the Procuratie Vecchie, and topped his building with a heavy attic fronted by statues to bring it up to the height of the Procuratie Vecchie. The Ala Napoleonica contains the entrance to the Museo Correr (see entry).

Arsenale (Arsenal)   N/O/P 4/5

The Arsenal was the Shipyard of Venice – until the end of the 17th c. the largest and busiest in the world. Founded in 1104, it was continuously expanded and in its heyday employed as many as 16,000 workmen. The Arsenal was a prohibited area and accessible by one land and one sea approach only. Every workman was privy to its secrets and, therefore, subject to security checks, which was how the Republic managed to keep its art of shipbuilding secret until about 1550.

Location
Rio del Arsenale

Quay
Arsenale

The entire Arsenal is still a closed military area without public access.

The landward entrance (Ingresso di Terra) is a triumphal arch in the Renaissance style. The lions on each side of the entrance come from Greece, booty brought back by Francesco Morosoni in the 17th c. after the reconquest of the Peloponnese. Of the two lions on the left, the larger one stood guard over the port of Piraeus while its fellow stood on the road from Athens to Eleusis.

★★Basilica di San Marco (Basilica of St Mark)   K/L 5

The Basilica of St Mark was the spiritual centre of the Republic; a splendid building for the Patron Saint of the Republic, the church of the Doge and State.

Location
Piazza di
San Marco

Quay
San Marco

Originally the palace chapel of the Doge, it became important in 829 when the remains of St Mark were transferred to Venice from Alexandria and

◄ *Monument to Condottiere Colleoni*

interred in the Cappella di San Marco, which 150 years later in 976, was destroyed by fire but soon rebuilt. Its present ground-plan, which is derived from the Church of the Apostles at Constantinople, dates from 1063 and consists of a Greek cross, covered by five domes, with two side-aisles on the west arm pointing towards the Piazza di San Marco (see entry). In 1094 the basilica was consecrated in the presence of the Emperor Henry IV and was raised to the status of official state church.

Three Procurators were appointed "Custodians of St Mark" to supervise the building and maintenance (see Procuratie). In the following centuries they supervised structural alterations to the basilica and its decoration; the mosaics were done in the 12th and 13th c. The 13th c. also saw the raising of the outer domes, the construction of the portico on the façade, the vaulting of the west porch, the installation of the bronze horses and the addition of the Byzantine parts of the Pala d'Oro. In the 14th c. the upper part of the façade and the domes were decorated in Gothic fashion and the pulpits and the Baptistery constructed. Further embellishments followed in the 15th–16th c. (altars, font, mosaics) and in the 17th–19th c. (mosaics).

The whole of Venice was legally compelled to take part in the rich furnishing of the State church. In 1075 the Doge Domenico Selvo passed a law that obliged all returning ships to bring back something precious to decorate the "House of St Mark", which is why today the basilica boasts over 500 columns of rare marble, porphyry, alabaster and jasper brought back from the East and Asia minor. The interior is clad with 4240 sq.m/45,622 sq.ft of gold mosaics, mostly 12th/13th c. Between 1500 and 1750, however, some of the venerable old sections were replaced by "modern" mosaics designed by artists including Titian and Tintoretto.

Exterior

North façade
This façade, facing the Piazzetta dei Leoncini, contains in the last arch the Porta dei Fiori, the Door of the Flowers, which merits close examination. Its relief depicts the Nativity (13th c.), framed by foliage, angels and Prophets.

Also worth noting are two other reliefs (towards the Piazza): the Etoimasia (7th–8th c.) depicts the throne of the Judge with six sheep on each side

Basilica of St Mark: façade facing the Piazzetta

San Marco: mosaic of the Last Judgment over the central portal

(symbolising the Twelve Apostles). The other relief shows Alexander the Great whose chariot is being drawn upwards by two griffins (10th c.).

West façade
The main façade on the Piazza is divided into five huge doorways. Over the portals is a terrace with a balustrade and above that five blind arches decorated with mosaics and topped by the Evangelists in gilded towers. Late Gothic ornamentation and figures. Above the central arch the so-called "Angel Staircase" leads up to the Patron Saint, St Mark. Behind the façade are the lead-covered domes.

The most remarkable of the mosaics decorating the portals is the one in the portal on the extreme left which dates from the 13th c. and depicts the Translation of the Body of St Mark to the Basilica.

The other mosaics are from the 17th and 18th c. and the Last Judgment over the centre portal dates only from 1836.

The central arch and the panels of the doors are richly decorated with reliefs and sculptures

Gallery
Until 1981 the four world-famous bronze horses stood on the gallery. The horses were once part of a quadriga in the Hippodrome (ancient race-course) of Constantinople. The date of their origin is still questionable; formerly they were thought to be the work of the 4th or 3rd c. B.C. (sculpted by Lysippos?). Recent research by British scientists ascribes them to the 3rd or 4th c. A.D. In 1204 they formed part of the booty brought to Venice by the Doge, Enrico Dandolo after the fall of Constantinople. In 1797 Napoleon carried them off to Paris and they were returned to Venice in 1815. They can now be seen in the Museo Marciano (see below).

Opening times
Mon.–Sat.
9.45am–5pm;
Sun. and
public holidays
4–5pm

Admission charge

Pietra del Bando
This "Stone of Banishment" at the south-west corner of the façade is another spoil of conquest; from this stump of porphyry column the decrees of the Republic were promulgated.

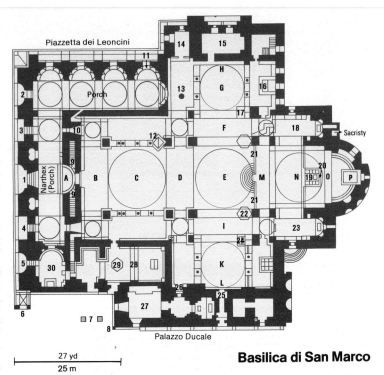

Basilica di San Marco

The **Basilica di San Marco** was begun in 830, rebuilt in 976 after a fire and remodelled in the 11th c. on the Byzantine pattern. The building inside measures 76·5 m (240·9 ft) by 51·8 m (169·9 ft) and is in the shape of a Greek cross. It has five domes. The interior is impressive for the beauty of its architecture, the changing views through the building and the magnificent mosaics.

 1 Main portal
2–5 Portal recesses
 6 Pietra del Bando
 7 Pilastri Acritani
 8 Sculpture of the Tetrarchs
 9 Stairs up to the Museo Marciano
10 Porta di San Pietro
11 Porta dei Fiori
12 Capitello del Crocifisso (Capital of the Cross)
13 Romanesque stoup with angels (12th c.)
14 Cappella della Madonna dei Mascoli
15 Cappella di Sant'Isidoro
16 Cappella della Madonna Nicopeia

17 Altare di San Pietro
18 Cappella di San Pietro
19 High Altar
20 Pala d'Oro
21 Iconostasis
22 Reliquary
23 Cappella di San Clemente
24 Altare di San Giacomo
25 Passage to the Doges' Palace
26 Entrance to the Treasury
27 Tesoro (Treasury), with goldsmiths' work, etc.
28 Battistero (Baptistery)
29 Font dating from 1546
30 Cappella Zen, named after Cardinal G. B. Zen (d. 1501)

MOSAICS
A Arch of Paradise
B Arch of the Apocalypse
C Scenes of Pentecost
D Scenes from the Passion
E The Ascension
F St Michael with sword
G St John
H Mary's family tree
I The Washing of the Feet, Temptation in the Wilderness
K St Leonard
L Four miracles of Jesus
M St Peter, The Resurrection, etc.
N Choir mosaics
O Lamb of God
P Christ in Majesty, with Saints

Flagpoles
The three huge cedar flagpoles in front of the façade were erected here in 1376 and their rich bronze bases were cast by Alessandre Leopardi in 1505.

The base of the middle flagpole has reliefs depicting Justice, Strength (an elephant) and Plenty. The southern flagpole base represents Venice's hegemony on land, and the northern one represents the Republic's hegemony at sea.

South façade
Until 1503, when this façade was enclosed, it was intended to be an imposing ceremonial entrance facing the lagoon, with a large door leading into the atrium (left) and the Baptistery (right).

Besides the two griffins (in the first arch) it is worth noting a Byzantine mosaic of the Virgin (13th c.) between the arches of the upper floor, in front of which nowadays two lamps are kept burning; at the time of the Republic black tallow candles were lit to comfort those under sentence of death who were executed in front of the Colonne di Marco e Teodora (see entry) on the Molo.

Pilastri Acritani
In front of the façade are two marble pilasters with magnificent reliefs (6th c.) Also the spoils of war, these were carried off by the Venetians in 1256 from the port of Acre.

Tetrarchs
The sculpture of the Tetrarchs (on the corner adjoining the Doge's Palace) is also world-famous. It was hewn from porphyry, probably in Egypt in the 4th c., and is thought to depict the Tetrarchs Diocletian, Maximilian, Constantius and Valerius, who together ruled the Roman Empire in A.D. 285.

Porch
Like all Byzantine basilicas St Mark's has a porch (narthex). The mosaics of the domes and arches are 13th c. (1220–1300); the only later addition was the "St Mark" inserted in the vaulting above the portal recess in 1545. Starting near the Zen Chapel and going north they depict the Creation, the story of Cain and Abel, the Building of Noah's Ark, the Building of the Tower of Babel, the stories of Abraham, Joseph and Moses.

Three portals lead to the interior of the church. All three are flanked by marble columns with richly ornamented capitals (6th–9th c.). The left portal shows Abraham with the three angels; the right portal has a bronze door covered in silver with an inscription in Greek (10th c.).

The middle portal, Venetian 12th c. work, was the main entrance to the church until 1064.

In the outer wall of the narthex are 12th c. tombs of the Doges.

The basic shape of the Basilica di San Marco is Byzantine, yet it is an astonishing mixture of styles containing elements of nearly every architectural form from classical to 19th c. Its form of building and its art treasures, acquired by such a diversity of means, have made the Basilica di San Marco one of the most important works of art in the world.

Interior of the Basilica

Four huge pillars bearing the domes and six columns with gilded capitals divide it into a nave and two aisles. Each of the five domes is almost 13m/43ft in diameter and has 16 windows. The sumptuous mosaics that cover the domes (over a total surface area of 4240 sq.m/45,622 sq.ft) fully justify its being popularly know as the "Basilica d'Oro" (Golden Basilica).

Domes
Before beginning to look round the church it is worth pausing to look at the dome mosaics, most of which date from between 1160 and 1200. Their chronological order begins in the east (above the choir), runs above the

Mosaics in San Marco

nave and finishes in the domes in the transept. The best view of the mosaics is from the galleries (anyone who is especially interested should take a telescope or binoculars). Access is from the inner portal.

Emanuel Dome
Christ, surrounded and venerated by Mary and the Prophets, giving a blessing.

Ascension Dome (centre)
Christ surrounded by stars; below, Mary between two cherubim and the Apostles.

Pentecost Dome
The dove of the Holy Ghost in the centre of a halo which extends to the Apostles around the edge of the dome; it symbolises the Holy Ghost entering into the Disciples.

Cappella di San Giovanni (north transept)
Mosaics showing the life of St John (1180).

Dome of St Leonard (south transept)
Mosaics depicting SS Leonard, Clement, Blasius and Nicholas (13th c.). The basilica had altars dedicated to these four saints.

Tour (clockwise)   Columned aedicula
The hexagonal columned aedicula has a pyramidal marble roof crowned by precious Oriental agate.

Another treasure is the Byzantine Crucifix from Constantinople

Cappella della Madonna dei Máscoli
The Chapel of the Madonna of Single Men has a fine stoup (12th c.) and Gothic altar sculptures which, like the mosaics of the vault ("The Death of Mary", etc.), date from the 15th c.

Cappella di Sant'Isidoro
The remains of the Saint were acquired by the unusual form of purchase in Chios in 1125 and interred in the chapel. The wall sarcophagus and the mosaics (mid 14th c.) depicting the life of St Isidore are worth seeing.

Cappella della Madonna Nicopeia
The most valuable item of decoration of the altar on the east side of the transept is the Byzantine icon of the Madonna Nicopeia ("the Bearer of Victory"). The icon, set with jewels, pearls and previous stones and in a delicate Byzantine enamel frame, was booty from Constantinople in 1204. The Madonna is greatly venerated by the Venetians.

Cappella di San Pietro
From the chapel there is a good view of the choir and the High Altar, and of the mosaics in the arches on the opposite side.

Rood-screen
In front of the choir (near the sacramental altar) is the intricate rood-screen. The lectern with the silver Crucifix and the statues of the Madonna and St Mark and the Apostles was the work of Jacopello and Pierpaolo delle Massegne (1394–1404). The rood-screen pulpit (right) was where the newly elected Doge was traditionally presented to the people.

Access
Cappella di San Clemente

Admission charge

Presbytery
The Presbytery was where the clergy, the Doge and the highest officials of Venice met on holy days (the basilica was a city church). The Doge's seat is no longer present however, and the original stalls have been replaced.

Choir platforms
The bronze reliefs by Jacopo Sansovino (1537–41) show scenes from the story of St Mark.

High Altar
The High Altar (1834–36) houses the relics of St Mark. Of interest are the four columns supporting the baldachin which are decorated with 324 reliefs (13th c.) showing scenes from the life of Jesus and Mary.

Pala d'Oro
San Marco's golden retable is the work of Byzantine and Venetian goldsmiths and enamellers who worked on it for 500 years. It is 3.45m/11½ft long and 1.4m/4½ft high.
    The oldest sections are the circular gold and enamel plates on the rim (c. 976).
    The enamel plates with episodes from the story of St Mark and scenes from the New Testament (1105) are Venetian, and the six large scenes of the life of Jesus (1209) are Byzantine.
    The middle panel with the figure of Christ in Majesty, the medallions with the Evangelists, the Twelve Apostles and the frame are also Venetian (13th c.)

Opening times
Mon.–Sat.
9.45am–5pm;
Sun. and
public holidays
2–5pm

Admission charge

Sacristy
The bronze door to the Sacristy is a masterpiece by Jacopo Sansovino (1486–1570). The reliefs show the Resurrection (top) the Entombment (bottom) and Saints and Prophets (at the sides). The heads are thought to be those of the artists Titian, Aretino, Palladio, Veronese and the Sansovino brothers.

Cappella di San Clemente
Noteworthy features in the former chapel of the Doge are the dividing wall of columns (late 14th c.), the mosaic of St Clement in the apse (12th c.) and the Holy Virgin on the altar.

Pala d'Oro

Tetrarchs embracing

Sacramental altar
The altar dates from 1617. In front of it is the place (marked by a mosaic in the floor) where the relics of St Mark were rediscovered after they had been lost in the fire of 976.

Tesoro
Opening times
Mon.–Sat.
9.45am–5pm;
Sun. and
public holidays
2–5pm

Admission charge

The Treasury is full of the precious objects brought to Venice by the Venetians after the sack of Constantinople in 1204 and which formed the basis of the now world-famous Treasure of San Marco.

Among the valuable objects captured in Constantinople were 110 Byzantine reliquaries made of gold and silver and set with previous stones (11th–13th c. work), Byzantine liturgical items, Byzantine icons made of gold and silver with reliefs and the traditional "Seal of St Mark" (c. 630). The sumptuous throne of the Doges (1500) is one of the few objects on display not brought to Venice as booty captured in war.

Battistero
The mosaics (14th c.) on the ceiling of the Baptistery depict the sending out of the Apostles ("Go out into the world and baptise all the peoples") and those on the walls show scenes from the life of St John the Baptist.

The font, thought to be by Sansovino, has bronze reliefs also showing the life of St John the Baptist. The figure of the Apostle comes from Segala (1556). Opposite the entrance is the tomb of Andrea Dandolo, the last Doge to be buried in San Marco.

Cappella Zen
The chapel houses the tomb of Cardinal Giambattista Zen. The bronze Madonna (1515) between St Mark and St John, called the "Madonna with the Shoe", is outstanding. According to the legend a poor man presented the Madonna with his left shoe which then turned to gold as a sign of heavenly gratitude.

The two red marble lions (*c.* 1200), Lombardy work, are also of interest.
The chapel was originally a room opening on to the Piazzetta and was the main entrance in the south façade.

Crypt
After seven years of restoration work, the crypt was reopened to the public in 1994. The hall of the crypt was built in the 11th c. and lies below sea level.

The Museum of San Marco (Museo Marciano) is entered by a small door near the main entrance to the church. Among the numerous exhibits in the church museum are: magnificent Gobelin tapestries (13th–16th c.), most of which are by Flemish artists; 12th c. Byzantine sculptures; mosaic fragments from the Baptistery (early 14th c.), as well as a very fine cover for the Pala d'Oro, made in 1345 by Paolo Veneziano and his sons, showing scenes from the life of St Mark. The four gilded copper horses previously on the gallery of San Marco are now housed in this museum.

Museo Marciano

Opening times
Daily 10am–5pm

Admission charge

Burano (Island)

The pretty little fishing village (pop. 6000) with painted houses and boats has been very well restored and is now the lagoon's artists' colony.
    Burano lace is famous; it is not made on bobbins but stitched. This art had been almost forgotten before it was revived in the early years of the 20th century.

Quay
Burano (from Fondamenta Nuove)

The Palazzo del Podestà (14th c.) contains the Scuola dei Merletti (Lace School) and a small museum with particularly fine pieces from various centuries (open Tues.–Sat. 9am–6pm, Sun. 10am–4pm. Admission charge).

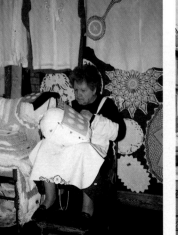

Lace making . . .   *. . . in Burano*

★ Ca' Foscari G 5

Location
Rio di Ca' Foscari/
Canal Grande

Quay
Ca' Rezzonico

The palace, today part of the university, is one of the most important Late Gothic buildings in Venice. When Doge Francesco Foscari (1423–57) ordered its building in the 15th c. it had four floors which was unknown at that time.

Foscari enlarged the mainland of the Venetian Republic in the west, but neglected to formulate policy in the east and was eventually forced in 1454 to sign a declaration surrendering the Eastern Mediterranean to the Turkish Sultan. In 1457, the year of his death, Foscari was overthrown by his opponents, the Loredani family, and his son Jacopo was banished.

In 1574 King Henry III of France used the palace as a residence. The main façade overlooks the Canal Grande.

★ Ca' da Mosto K 4

Location
Calle Postal/
Canal Grande

Quay
Ca' d'Oro

The palace dates back to the 12th c. and was built in the Venetian-Byzantine style. Alvise da Mosto, the first European to sail round Cape Verde in West Africa in 1465, was born in this house in 1432. Between the 16th and the 18th c. the Ca' da Mosto housed the well-known Leon Bianco (White Lion) Hotel. In 1769 and 1775 the German Emperor and son of Maria Theresa, Joseph II, lived here during his stay in Venice.

The main façade overlooks the Canal Grande.

★ Ca' d'Oro with the Galleria Franchetti (Golden House) J 3

Location
Canal Grande

This palace is Venetian Gothic at its most perfect. Originally richly painted and gilded – hence its name – it has lost its gilding but the marble filigree-

Ca' d'Oro: Highpoint of Venetian Architecture

work of Bartolomeo Bon (who also built the Porta della Carta in the Palazzo Ducale (see entry) dating from between 1421 and 1440 is still of unrivalled beauty. The interior provides a vivid impression of how Venetian nobles lived in the late Middle Ages. The mosaic on the ground floor, a copy of the one in the basilica of St Mark, is also worth seeing.

There is a red marble well in the courtyard with allegories of Strength, Justice and Mercy.

The palace houses the Galleria Franchetti art collection, given to the State in 1922 by the saviour of the Ca' d'Oro, Baron Giorgio Franchetti. Extensive restoration work (1969–84) has not altered the character of the private collection. The exhibits do not give the impression of being in a museum, but rather complement the historical setting of the palace.

Among the many fine paintings of various schools are Titian's "Venus before the Mirror", "Venus and Cupid" by Paris Bordone (16th c.), "Portrait of a Nobleman" by van Dyck (1622–27) and the unfinished "St Sebastian" by Mantegna (c. 1500).

Marble busts, bronzes and terracottas by Bernini, Giambologna, Tullio Lombardo, Ricci, etc. complete the collection. In addition there are fragments of frescoes by Giorgione and Titian which once adorned the façade of the Fondaco dei Tedeschi (see entry).

Quay
Ca' d'Oro

Opening times
Daily 9am–1.30pm

Admission charge

★Ca' Venier dei Leoni e Collezione Peggy Guggenheim   H/J 6
(Venier House of the Lions and Peggy Guggenheim Collection)

The palace, only a few steps away from the Church of Santa Maria della Salute (see entry) and the Palazzo Corner della Ca' Grande (see entry), was begun in 1749. It was never completed, however, and has only one floor. The aristocratic Venier family are said to have kept lions in the sleepy garden – hence the appellation "dei Leoni" (of the Lions).

Location
Canal Grande/
Fondamenta Venier

Quay
Salute, Accademia

F. Léger: "City People"   J. Metzinger: "Cycle Track"

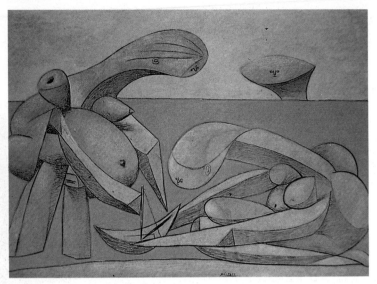

Pablo Picasso: "On the Seashore"

Opening times
Mon., Wed.–Sun.
11am–6pm

Admission charge

The American Peggy Guggenheim (1884–1979) opened a museum of contemporary art in London in 1939, and in 1942 the "Art of the Century" Gallery in New York from which her private Venetian collection of cubist, abstract and surrealist paintings is derived. In 1948 Peggy Guggenheim first exhibited her collection at the Bienniale in Venice. Shortly afterwards the Ca' Venier dei Leoni became her new residence and here she opened her collection to the public. Today the collection belongs to the Salomon R. Guggenheim foundation in New York set up by Peggy's uncle, but with the proviso that the works of art should remain as a museum in Venice.

The collection includes works by Max Ernst, to whom Peggy Guggenheim was married ("The Kiss", 1927), Pablo Picasso ("On the Beach", 1937), Georges Braques ("Clarinet", 1912), Fernard Leger ("City People", 1919), Jean Metzinger ("Cycle Track", c. 1914), Joan Miro ("Dutch Interior II", 1928), Salvador Dali ("The Birth of Liquid Desires", 1931/32), Paul Klee ("Portrait of Mrs. P in the South", 1924), Rene Magritte ("The Voice of Space", 1931), Alberto Giacometti ("Woman on Foot", 1932), Constantin Brancusi ("Maiastra", c. 1912), Piet Mondrian ("Composition", 1938/39), Marc Chagall ("Rain", 1911), and Jackson Pollock ("Moonwoman", 1942). On the terrace looking on to the Canal Grande stands Marino Marini's equestrian statue "Angel of the City" (1948).

★Campanile   K 5

Location
Piazza di San Marco

Quay
San Marco

Opening times
9.30am–7pm daily

Admission charge

The Piazza di San Marco (see entry) would not be complete without the rectangular towering Campanile in front of the Procuratie Nuove (see entry) that links the Piazza and the Piazzetta (see entry).

The Campanile was begun in the 10th c.; it was completed in the 12th c. and its pointed roof added in the 15th c. It could be seen from afar by approaching ships and it guided them home with its gilded pinnacle.

It collapsed on July 14th 1902, smashing the Loggetta (see entry) at its foot but causing no casualties. By 1912 it had been painstakingly rebuilt.

The Campanile is 98.6m/322½ft high and has a double wall. A lift goes up to the Belfry from where there is a magnificent view of the city.

In the Middle Ages the Campanile was also used as a pillory: wrong-doers – including adulterers and renegade priests – were closeted in a cage and hoisted half-way up the tower. This breezy punishment could last for several weeks.

I Carmini (officially: Santa Maria del Carmine; church)   F 5

The Gothic church with the tall 17th c. Campanile dates from the 13th to the 14th c. Like the Scuola dei Carmini (see entry), it belonged to the Carmelites.

Location
Campo Carmini

The interior has some very fine paintings, several in the nave showing scenes from the history of the Order. The "Adoration of the Shepherds" (early 16th c.), one of Cima da Conegliano's most highly prized works, is at the second side-altar on the right, and Lorenzo Lotto's "St Nicholas and Saints" (early 16th c.) is in the left-hand aisle.

Quay
Ca' Rezzonico

Chiesa dell'Angelo Raffaele (Church of the Archangel Raphael)   E 6

This church was founded as early as the 7th c. but the present building, which is rather austere, dates from the 17th c.

Location
Campo San
Sebastiano

Inside in the organ-loft is a series of pictures depicting the story of Tobias. These important 18th c. paintings are by one of the Guardi brothers, but it is not clear whether the artist was Giovanni Antonio Guardi or his younger brother Francesco.

Quay
Ca' Rezzonico

★Chiesa dei Gesuati (officially: Santa Maria del Rosario; church)   G/H 6

In the 15th c. the church belonged to the Guild of the Poveri Gesuati (whose name it has retained) but was taken over by the Dominicans who had the present building erected in 1726–36 by the master-builder Giorgio Massari. It is a gem of 18th c. Venetian architecture; a large room with side-chapels and a façade reminiscent of Palladio.

Location
Fondamenta
Zattere
dei Gesuati

There are ceiling frescoes by Giambattista Tiepolo – "The Ascent into Heaven of St Dominic", "The Introduction of the Rosary by Mary", "St Dominic giving a Blessing", and the painting "Madonna in Glory".

Quay
Accademia

The altar-pieces "St Dominic" (c. 1743; second altar on the right) and "Dominicans" (third altar on the right) are by Piazzetta; Sebastiano Ricci was responsible for the altar-piece "Pope Pius V and Saints" (c. 1732–34; first altar on the left) and Tintoretto painted "The Crucifixion" (third altar on the left).

★Chiesa degli Scalzi   F 3
(officially: Santa Maria di Nazareth; Church of the Discalced)

The church is a fine Baroque building erected between 1670 and 1680 by Baldassare Longhena. Its façade was added between 1683 and 1689 by Guiseppe Sardi. The building is famed for its many sculptures. In the second chapel on the right is Tiepolo's fresco "The Glory of St Teresa", and the third chapel on the left contains his fresco "Christ praying in the garden of Gethsemane".

Location
Lista di Spagna

Quay
Ferrovia
(railway station)

The ceiling fresco by Tiepolo was destroyed by an Austrian grenade during the First World War. The present ceiling fresco is the work of Ettore Tito (1934).

★ Chioggia

Location
45km/28 miles
south of Venice

Quay
Chioggia, ship
and bus: service
11 from Riva degli
Schiavoni or Lido

Near the southern end of the Venice lagoon (S.S 309 "Strada Roma" from Marghera) lies the lively island town of Chioggia (alt. 2m/6½ft; pop. 50,000), once the centre of Venetian salt production. The town was destroyed by the Genoese in 1379 and is now a flourishing fishing port.

Chioggia attracts many visitors on account of its picturesque tumble-down streets, its canals, which are reminiscent of those of Venice, and its colourful bohemian life. At the beginning of the Corso del Popolo, the principal thoroughfare which is filled with cafés, restaurants and shops, stand the Cathedral, restored by B. Longhena, the 14th c. Campanile (64m/210ft high) and the little Gothic church of San Martino (1392). Opposite San Martino is the house where the painter Rosalba Carriera (1675–1757) was born. In the mid 1880s Venice's famous playwright Carlo Goldini (see Famous People) lived in Chioggia. In his comedy "Baruffechiozzote" he portrayed the citizens of the town in a most amusing way.

Sottomarina

A bridge, 800m/½ mile long, leads from the Old Town of Chioggia to the popular seaside suburb of Sottomarina (alt. 2m/6½ft).

Albarella

Some 20km/12 miles south-east of Sottomarina lies the island of Albarella in the Po delta. It is a holiday centre with many facilities for visitors, including tennis and riding centres, a golf-course and a marina.

Colonne di Marco e Teodoro (Columns of St Mark and St Theodore) L 5

Location
Molo

Quay
San Marco

Doge Michieli actually brought three columns back from Tyre (now in the Lebanon) in 1125, but when they were being unloaded one of them fell into the sea and sank to the bottom of the lagoon.

The other two were set up on the Molo. One of them was crowned with the Lion of St Mark – probably an early medieval mythical animal from Persia that had been given wings and a book between its paws. Until the 18th c. the lion was gilded. St Theodore was set up on the second column; he was the first Patron Saint of Venice until superseded by St Mark. The gleaming white statue has been skilfully assembled: the head belongs to a Roman Emperor and the rest, including the dragon, to an early St George.

Dogana di Mare (Old Customs House) K 6

Location
Punta della
Dogana

Quay
Salute

The Customs House was built by G. Benoni between 1676 and 1682 when the Senate hoped they could halt the decline in the Venetian economy by enforcing rigorous customs regulations. On the tip of the spire is a weather-vane of Fortuna", seen standing on a gilded globe supported by two telamones.

Doges' Palace

See Palazzo Ducale

★ Fondaco dei Tedeschi (German Commodity Exchange) K 4

Location
Ponte di Rialto
(access)

The Fondaco (from the Arabic "funduk" = commodity exchange) dei Tedeschi, the German Commodity Exchange is first recorded in 1228. At that time the "German" merchants also included Poles, Czechs and Hungarians.

Fondaco dei Tedeschi

Today the building contains the main Post Office. When the Fondaco burned down in 1505 the Republic assumed the cost of rebuilding it and entrusted the decoration of the façade (and its vanished frescoes) to Giorgione and Titian.

Quay
Rialto

The fragments of its remaining frescoes can be seen in the Ca' d'Oro (see entry). The prime position close to the Rialto and the fact that Venice had paid for rebuilding, underlined the economic advantages which the Republic obtained from this institution. On every purchase and sale – these generally involved considerable sums – a high commission had to be paid to the state of Venice. It was not for nothing that in the 16th and 17th c. the Fondaco was called "the golden ark of the Senate".

The exchange was both a place of business and a refuge for the merchants. They were not permitted to appear alone, nor to conduct any business outside the Fondaco. They were subjected to strict controls, they lived and ate communally (no women were allowed) and they were subjected to Venetian supervision. Publically the German merchants were presented as a "brotherhood" of the Church of San Bartolomeo (see entry) which belonged to them.

The façade on the Canal Grande is, in accordance with Venetian tradition, in three sections. The middle section is a five-arched "Portico"; above this are the dining-rooms on the corners of the upper floor, topped by an ornamental merlon-like moulding.

The architecture of the building corresponds exactly to the purpose for which it served: 160 rooms are spread over four floors surrounding a courtyard. The shops were in the outer rooms of the ground floor while the other rooms were used for storage. The rooms of the upper floors were living quarters and offices. The Customs post overlooked the canal.

★Fondaco dei Turchi e Museo di Storia Naturale   H 3
(Turkish Commodity Exchange and Natural History Museum)

Location
Fondamenta dei
Megio/Rio Fortego
dei Turchi

Quay
San Staè

Opening times
Tues.–Sun.
9am–1pm

Closed
Mon.

Admission charge

The building, originally a palace, dates from the 9th c. and is one of the oldest in Venice. It has existed in its present form since the mid 13th c. In the 14th and 15th c. it was the residence in Venice of the Dukes of Ferrara. Emperor Friedrich III stayed here as their guest in 1452 and 1469.

From 1608 to 1621 the Emperor's Ambassador, Georg Fugger, had his office in this palace.

In 1621 the Council of the Republic allocated the building to the Turkish merchants for use as living accommodation and as a warehouse (hence the appellation "Fondaco"). At the beginning of the 19th c. the palace was totally in ruins, so the city took it over and after 1858 rebuilt it in its original 13th c. style; since 1880 it has been used as a museum, and today is an outstanding example of the Byzantine-Venetian mixture of styles common in the 13th c.

The building currently houses the Natural History Museum (Museo di Storia Naturale).

The museum gives a good idea of the animal life in the Adriatic, but its impressive array of exhibits also covers other marine areas. The associated lapidary and general zoological collections are well worth seeing.

The ground floor also contains a notable exhibition of Venetian well-heads.

★★I Frari (officially: Santa Maria Gloriosa dei Frari; church)   G 4/5

Location
Campo dei Frari

This Gothic church was begun by the Franciscans ("Frari" in Venetian = "Frati" in Italian) about 1340. The façade, interior, annexes, Cappella Emi-

Turkish Commodity Exchange

Santa Maria Gloriosa dei Frari

© Baedeker

1 Main portal
2 Tomb of Alvise.
Pasqualigo († 1528)
3 Tomb of Pietro Bernardo
(† 1538)
4 Tomb of Girolamo Garzoni
(1688)
5 Crucifixion altar
6 Holy water basin with
statuettes by
G. Campagna (1593)
7 Tomb of A. Canova
(† 1822)
8 Monument to Titian
(† 1576)
9 Tomb of Doge Giovanni
Pesaro († 1659)
10 Altar of Purification
11 "Madonna di Ca Pesaro"
Titian (1526)
12 Tomb of Bishop Iacopo
Pesaro († 1547)

13 Altar of St Joseph of
Copertino
14 Altar of St Catherine
15 Choirstalls of 1468.
16 Monument to Genero
Orsini
17 Tomb of General I.
Marcello († 1484)
18 Tomb of Beato Pacifico
Buon († 1437)
19 Tomb of Doge Francesco
Foscari († 1457)
20 Tomb of Doge Niccolò
Tron († 1473)
21 High altar with Titian's
"Assumption of the
Madonna" ("Assunta",
1516–18)
22 "Madonna Enthroned
with Saints" by G. Bellini
(1488)
23 Chapter House
24 Trinity Fountain (1713–14,
G Trognon)
25 Refectory

A Bell Tower

CHAPELS
B Emiliani
C Corner: Marble statue of
John the Baptist (1554);
altarpiece by Bart. Vivarini
(1474)
D Milanesi: Tomb of Claudio
Monteverdi († 1643);
altarpiece by Al. Vivarini
E Trevisan: Melchiore
Trevisan († 1500)
F San Francesco
G Fiorentini: wooden statue
of John the Baptist by
Donatello (1451)
H Sacramento: Wall-tomb of
the Florentine Ambassador
Duccio degli Alberti
(† 1336)
I Bernado: Altar painting by
Bart. Vivarini (1482)

I Frari

Interior

liana and Cappella Cornaro were added in the middle of the 15th c. The simple unadorned interior corresponds to the ideals of the Franciscan monks. The impressive Campanile (14th c.) is the second highest in the city.

Opening times: Mon.–Sat. 9.30–11.45am and 2.30–6pm, Sun. and public holidays 3–6pm.

Among the outstanding works of art in the church are:
North aisle
Mausoleum of A. Canova
The mausoleum was made by the pupils of the sculptor Antonio Canova (1757–1822). It contains only his heart, his body having been buried in his native town of Possagno.

Mausoleum of Doge Giovanni Pesaro
The mausoleum for Doge Giovanni Pesaro is the work of the sculptor Baldassare Longhens.

"Madonna di Ca' Pesaro"
This painting, completed in 1526, is one of Titian's most important works.

Cappella Emiliani
The chapel has a very fine polyptych with marble figures (mid 15th c.).

Left transept
Cappella Cornaro
The statue of St John the Baptist on the stoup was created by the sculptor and master-builder Jacopo Sansovino (c. 1550). He more than anyone else left his mark on the townscape of Venice and created masterpieces in the field of interior decoration.

Cappella Milonese
In this chapel is an inscribed stone marking the grave of Claudio Monteverdi (1567–1643), the pioneer of opera; the retable "St Ambrose with Saints" and "Coronation of the Virgin" was begun by Alvise Vivarini and completed by Marco Basaiti.

Sanctuary
The Sanctuary contains the tomb of the Doges Francesco Foscari (1423–47) and Niccolò Tron (1471–73) by Antonio Rizzo. Of especial note is Titian's painting, created between 1516 and 1518, over the High Altar, the "Assunta" (Assumption of the Virgin). The painting is orientated upwards and is divided into three zones.

Right transept
Statue of St John the Baptist
The Florentine sculptor Donatello (c. 1386–1466) created this figure in wood in 1451 (first chapel to the right of the Sanctuary). It depicts St John the Baptist preaching – his mouth is open and his right hand raised in gesture.

Cappella Bernardo
In the third chapel to the right of the Sanctuary is a triptych, "Madonna with Child and Saints", dating from 1482 by the Italian painter Bartolomeo Vivarini.

The Sacristy
The Triptych "The Madonna and Child Enthroned with four Saints". The painting, a gift from the Pesaro family, is by Giovanni Bellini. It depicts the Patron Saint of Pietro Pesaro (father), Niccolò, Marco and Benedetto (sons).

I Frari: Titians "Assumption of the Virgin Mary" ("Assunto") ▶

Basilica: I Frari

Donatello: St John the Baptist

Nave
Monastic Choir
The choir is an outstanding example of the wood-carving of Marco Cozzi.

South aisle
"St Jerome"
The marble statue by Alessandro Vittoria dates from 1560. The stone in the Saint's hand refers to his self-castigation. Jerome lived as a hermit for a time.

Mausoleum of Titian
This was a gift from Ferdinand I of Austria, king of Lombardy Veneto, and is the work of the Zandomeneghi brothers (1852).

★★Galleria dell'Accademia (Academy of Fine Arts)   H 6

Location
Canal Grande/Pora dell'Accademia (access)

Quay
Accademia

Opening times
daily 9am–7pm

Admission charge

The Galleria dell'Accademia, called "Accademia" for short, is on the Canal Grande near the Ponte dell'Accademia (see entry). It has the most important and comprehensive collection of 15th–18th c. Venetian painting in existence.

The basis of the collection was the Accademia di Belle Arti founded in 1750 by the painter Giovanni Battista Piazzetta. Since 1807 it has been housed in the former Monastery of Santa Maria della Carità (1441), and the Scuola di Santa Maria della Carità (15th c.) and the adjacent monastery buildings of the Lateran Canons (c. 1500).

Church, monastery and school were secularised about 1800. In 1802 private art-lovers set up a temporary depot in the empty rooms for works of art that had become "homeless" after the closure on monasteries and churches and the clearing of the palaces of noble families. In a very short time a unique gallery was assembled in this way, and was steadily enlarged by purchases and donations.

Room 1: This room formerly belonged to the Scuola di Santa Maria della Carità and has a richly carved and gilded ceiling (15th c.). It contains works by masters of Venetian Gothic painting such as Paolo Veneziano, Lorenzo Venesiano, Michele Giambono, Antonio Vivarini and Jacobello del Fiore.

Room 2: 15th and 16th c. Renaissance painting. "Madonna and Saints" by Giovanni Bellini (1430–1516), "The Garden of Gethsemane" by Marco Basaiti, "Portrait of Christ" by Vittore Carpaccio and "Madonna under the Orange Tree" by Cima da Conegliano.

Room 3: 16th c. Venetian panel-paintings.

Room 4: Paintings from the second half of the 15th c. "St George" by Andrea Mantegna, "St Jerome and a Donor" bu Piero della Francesca, "Madonna and Child" by Cosmè Tura and works by Giovanni Bellini.

Room 5: "Sacra Conversazione" – also called "Madonna Giovanelli" – by Giovanni Bellini and five panels with allegories; works by the Venetian painter Giogione: "Tempèsta" (probably the master's best-known work) and "Old Woman".

Room 6: "Fishermen presenting St Mark's Ring to the Doge" by Paris Bordone, "Banquet of Dives" by Bonifacio de' Pitati and "St John the Baptist" by Titian.

Room 7: "Gentleman in his Study" by the Venetian painter Lorenzo Lotto.

Room 8: Palma the Elder's "Sacra Conversazione".

Room 9: Paintings by Fr. Vecellio and works by the school of Tintoretto.

Room 10: Scenes by Jacopo Tintoretto from the Life of St Mark, including "The Miracle of St Mark"; "Supper in the House of Levi" by Paolo Veronese and the magnificent "Pietà" by Titian.

J. Tintoretto: "Procurator Jacopo Soranzo"

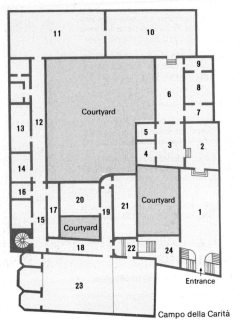

Galleria dell'Accademia

ROOMS
1 14th–15th c. panel-painting
2 15th–16th c. Venetian Renaissance altar-pieces
3 16th c. Venetian panel-paintings
4 Second half of 15th c.
5 G. Bellini, Giorgione
6 16th c. Venetian painting
7 Lorenzo Lotto
8 Palma the Elder
9 school of Tintoretto.
10 16th c. Venetian masters including Veronese, Tintoretto and Titian
11 Tintoretto, Bassano, Tiepolo, Veronese, Giordano, Da Cortona
12 Corridor: 18th c. landscapes
13 16th c. Venetian painting
14 Early 17th c.
15 Corridor: Tiepolo, Pellegrini
16 18th c. Venetian painting
17 Small 18th c. paintings
18 18th c. paintings
19 19th c. panel-paintings
20 "Miracles of the Relic of the True Cross"
21 Vittore Carpaccio's "Legend of St Ursula"
22 Paintings from the first half of the 18th c.
23 Former monastery church: G. Bellini, A. and B. Vivarini, Cima da Conegliano
24 Former Hall of the Scuola della Carità: A. Vivarini, Titian, etc.

Room 11: Several works by Jacopo Tintoretto, including "Cain and Abel"; the "Marriage of St Catherine" by Paolo Veronese, and works by the Italian painters Giabattista Tiepolo, Luca Giordano and Pietro da Cortona.

Room 12: 18th c. Venetian landscapes.

Room 13: Works by 16th c. Venetian painters including Jacopo Bassano and Jacopo Tintoretto.

Room 14: 17th c. Italian painters, including Bernardo Strozzi, Domenico Fetti and the German painter Johann Liss.

Room 15: Two paintings with religious themes by Giandomenico Tiepolo (son of Giambattista Tiepolo).

Rooms 16–19: Early works by Giambattista Tiepolo (18th c.), "The Fortune Teller" by Giovanni Battista Piazzetta (a major work), and paintings by Francesco Guardi and Giovanni Antonio Canaletto (see Famous People). Genre-painting by Pietronghi, pastel portraits by the Venetian-born Rosalba Carriera and models by Antonio Canova.

Room 20: This room contains paintings from the Scuola di San Giovanni Evangelista, including the work of Gentile Bellini, Vittore Carpaccio, Giovanni Mansueti, Lazzaro Bastiani, etc.
    All paintings relate to the miracles of the relic of the True Cross (1494–1501). This relic of the True Cross is still kept in the Scuola.

Room 21: A series of paintings of the legend of St Ursula (Martyrdom of the Breton princess) by Vittore Carpaccio (late 15th c.).

Enthroned Madonna by N. di Pietro   *Mary Magdalen by G. Bellini*

Room 22: Corridor with Neo-Classical pictures.

Room 23: This room was part of the former Monastery Church of Santa Maria della Carità. It contains 15th and 16th c. paintings by G. Bellini, Alvise and Bartolomeo Vivarini, Cima da Conegliano, etc.

Room 24: Former Hall of the Scuola della Corità. It contains "The Presentation of the Virgin at the Temple" and the "Mourning of Christ" by Titian, and a Byzantine-Venetian reliquary.

Galleria d'Arte Moderna

See Palazzo Pesaro

Galleria Franchetti

See Ca' d'Oro

★I Gesuiti (officially: Santa Maria Assunta; church)   K/L 3

The church, dating from the 13th c., was sumptuously rebuilt between 1714 and 1729 by Domenico Rossi in the Roman Baroque style for the Jesuits.

Location
Campo Gesuiti

With its barrel-vaulted single nave, side-chapels, transept and choir, the church has an imposing and elaborate interior: walls clad with green and white marble, massive pillars and colonnades, gilding, and a High Altar with a baldachin and sculptured retable.

Quay
Ca' d'Oro

I Gesuiti

Grounds of the Ghetto Nuovo

The most magnificent of the paintings is Titian's "Martyrdom of St Laurence" (between 1558 and 1560, last chapel on the left). Also noteworthy are Tintoretto's "Assumption of the Virgin" (in the left transept) and wall- and ceiling-paintings by Palma the Younger in the Sacristy.

Il Ghetto e Museo della Comunità Israelitica   G/H 2
(Ghetto and Jewish Museum)

Location
Campo Ghetto
Nuovo

Quay
Ferrovia

Opening times
Scuola Grande
Tedesca and
Jewish
Museum:
Mon.–Fri.,
Sun.10am–4pm

Closed
Sat. and Jewish
holy days

From 1090 Jews, who were not allowed into Venice itself, settled on the island of Spinalonga, later named Giudecca (see entry).

In 1395 the Jews quarrelled with the Christian population and had to leave Giudecca for Mestre.

In 1509, during the war against the League of Cambrai, they fled the flames of Mestre for the island city.

In 1516 the Senate allocated the site of a former iron-foundry, The Ghetto Nuovo, to the German and Italian Jews for living quarters. In 1541 the Jews arriving from the East were settled in the Ghetto Vecchio. The word "ghetto" is said to be derived from "gettare" – to cast in metal – and this district was named after the original foundries.

In 1633 this enclosed Jewish quarter was enlarged to include the Ghetto Nuovissimo (the "newest" ghetto).

The Jews were allowed only limited freedom of movement in the city, they had to wear red or yellow hats and were not allowed to acquire land. The gates of the ghetto remained locked from dusk until dawn. Infringements were punished by the Senate with large fines.

As decreed by the Senate, Jews were mostly dealers in second-hand goods and – subsequently – doctors.

Space was at a premium in the ghetto so that houses as high as seven or eight storeys are not uncommon. The façades are plain, almost shabby.

It is, however, worth going inside the synagogues:

The Scuola Grande Tedesca (The Great German School) has been renovated and is now an intimate Baroque room with an oval gallery (an elegant way of compensating for the irregularity of the ground-plan) and some very fine individual pieces.

The Scuola Canton (Canton School) is the richly ornamented private house of prayer of the German-Jewish Canton family who made their fortune as bankers.

Another synagogue is the Scuola Italiana (Italian School).

The Scuola Levantina (Levantine School) is decorated with a pulpit by Andrea Brustolon (1662–1732).

The Scuola Spagnola (Spanish School) has a magnificent room created in the 17th c. by Baldassare Longhena, the most important exponent of the Venetian Baroque style (his best-known work is Santa Maria della Salute; see entry).

At the Campo de Ghetto Nuovo a memorial tablet and bronze reliefs commemorate 200 Jewish inhabitants who, between December 8th 1943 and August 17th 1944, were taken away to Nazi concentration camps and murdered.

Memorial tablet

It is also worth paying a visit to the Museo della Comunità Israelitica (Museum of the Jewish Community). This small but interesting museum, attached to the Scuola Granda Tedesca, contains objects used in worship, manuscripts and documents on the history of the Jews of Venice.

Museo della Comunità Israelitica

Giardinetto (park)   K 5/6

The Giardinetto, extending west of the Piazzetta (see entry) on the Molo, is one of those small parks which have grown up in Venice since the early 19th c. and which bring to the city a touch of green which many visitors find lacking.

Location
Molo

Quay
San Marco

Madam de Staël, for example, complained "An indefinable sadness creeps into the heart when one arrives in Venice. One is not in the country, for there is no green tree to be seen and yet not in the town, for every sound is drowned out by the water".

It was to another French visitor (and the one most unwelcome to the city) that Venice owed her parks. Beside the Giardini Pubblici (see entry) Napoleon I was also responsible for the Giardinetto behind the Procuratie Nuove (see entry) because he disliked having his view of the sea from the window of the Procuratie Nuove blocked by a grain store which stood there.

Giardini Pubblici (public gardens)   O 6, P 6/7, Q 7/8

The Giardini Pubblici were laid out by Napoleon I at the south-east end of the main island. Nowadays, however, much of the site is covered by the buildings which house the "Biennale", the biennial international art exhibition which takes place every two years. Nevertheless there is sufficient room for Rococo and 19th c. statues and for paths among the palms, acacias and plane trees.

Location
Riva dei Sette Martiri

Quay
Giardini

La Giudecca (island)   E–L 7/8

Quay
Sant'Eufemia,
Redentore, Zitelle
(Line 5 from Riva
degli Schiavoni,
Fondamenta delle
Zattere)

This island of Giudecca was inhabited by Jews from the Early Middle Ages. They were subsequently moved to Mestre and finally ended up in the Ghetto (see entry). The island, however, derives its name from the condemned people who were formerly banished here (Lat. indicare = to condemn).

The island is separated from the city by the broad Canal della Giudecca and divided into eight adjacent islands by small canals. Once a haven for Venetian nobles who had their villas here, today it is mostly inhabited by working-class families.

★Il Redentore (Church of the Redeemer)

Location
Campo Redentore

Quay
Redentore

The white Franciscan church is one of the principal works of the famous Italian architect Andrea Palladio (1508–80). He based his designs on ancient models, in particular on the ten books "De Architectura", said to be by the Roman architect Vitruvius Pollio of the time of the Emperor Augustus. As a result he based the façade of the Church of the Redeemer on three superimposed temple fronts. The double gable and attic were adopted from the Pantheon in Rome. The dominant dome forms the central part of the single-aisled hall church between the nave and the monastic choir.

A festival and the church owe their origin to an epidemic of plague in 1576. At that time the Senate vowed to build the church and to celebrate the Feast of the Redemption; the Franciscans undertook the religious obligations. The building of the church began in 1577 and was completed in 1592.

Palladio modelled the interior of the church on his earlier basilica of San Giorgio Maggiore (see entry), even though it is less ornate. On either side of the nave, the architecture of which is reminiscent of a Roman bath-house,

Church of Le Zitelle on the island of La Giudecca

Il Redentore

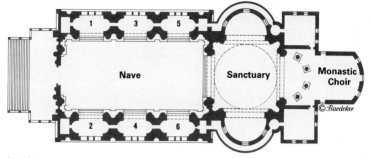

Altarpieces
1 "Transformation of Christ" (school of Tintoretto)
2 "Birth of Christ", Francesco Bassano
3 "Resurrection of Christ", Francesco Bassano
4 "Baptism of Christ", Veronese
5 "Internment of Jesus", Palmail Giovane
6 "Scourging of Christ" (school of Tintoretto)

are three semi-circular chapels. The altar reredoses portray scenes from the life of Christ. Of special interest are the "Baptism of Christ" from the workshop of Veronese, and the two altar wings, the "Scourging" and "Transfiguration of Christ" from the school of Tintoretto. Although the Late Baroque altar was not finished until 1680, the bronze Crucifixion group dates from the end of the 16th c. Like the high altar of S. Maria Maggiore it is a work by Girolamo Campagnas (1550–1623). Also notable is a painting of the Madonna by Alvise Vivarini.

After the dedication of the church the Doge came every year with the chief officials of the state to a thanksgiving service. The Venetians still make a pilgrimage here on the Feast of the Redemption (3rd Sunday in July) to thank the Saviour for the end of the epidemic. A bridge of boats is constructed from Zattere across the Giudecca Canal, over which the procession makes its way to the Church of the Redeemer. In the evening the festival concludes with a magnificent firework display and a procession of illuminated boats.

Le Zitelle (officially: Santa Maria della Presentazione; church)

The Church of the Madonna was also planned by Andrea Palladio. Although simpler and smaller than the Redentore it is still a fine building.

It dates from the 16th c. but has no works of art of any significance.

Location
Fondamenta della Zitelle

Quay
Zitelle

Libreria Vecchia di San Marco (Old Library)   K/L 5

The Old Library on the west side of the Piazzetta opposite the Palazzo Ducale (see entries) is the masterpiece of Sansovino, the architect and sculptor, who worked on it between 1536 and 1553. After his death it was completed by Vincenzo Scamozzi to the original specifications.

The library represents the real turning-point of Venetian architecture and the final break with Gothic Venice. Sansovino was a Florentine; he leaned towards the art of that region and towards Classical Rome. With this structure of Baroque-Roman arcades, arches, columns, balustrades and sculptures Venice lost its own individual form of architecture, since from then on almost all new buildings, especially the palaces, were modelled on this particular innovation. This style of architecture also became known

Location
Piazzetta

Quay
San Marco

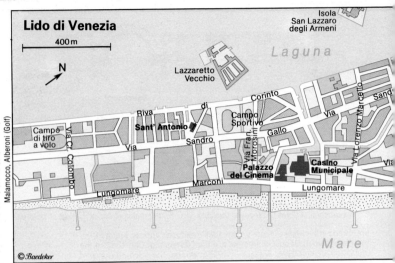

throughout Europe as a result of Scamossi's theoretical work "Idea dell'architettura universale" (Idea of a universal architecture) which appeared in 1615.

The library itself is a unique work of art, elegant, harmonious and yet majestic.

The building (plan on page 64) today contains the exhibition rooms of the Biblioteca Nazionale Marciana, the "Library of St Mark". An impressive central portal (1533–54) by Alessandro Vittoria gives on to the staircase with stuccoes also by Vittoria. The ceiling in the anteroom is adorned with "Fresco of Wisdom" by Titian (1560). The "Golden Hall" has 21 ceiling-medallions (three of them, "Geometry", Arithmetic" and "Music", by Veronese) and on the walls are twelve portraits of philosophers, five of them by Tintoretto.

The exhibition rooms contain an astonishing collection of gems, manuscripts, calligraphy and book illuminations, including the Grimaldi Breviary (1510–20) which alone has 831 pages of Flemish miniatures.

The actual library of St Mark with its 1,000,000 volumes is today housed in the former Mint (Zecca, 1536) which is connected to the exhibition rooms.

Lido (island)

Location
Santa Maria
Elisabetta (from
Riva Degli
Schiavoni)

Car ferry
from Venice–
Tronchetto

In previous centuries for Venetians the Lido only represented a trip into the country. Subsequently a fashionable resort, today it is a Mecca for tourists.

The island is 12km/7½ miles long, almost half of which is a beach of fine smooth sand. Apart from the usual bathing (each section of the beach belongs to one or several hotels), there are facilities for golf, tennis, horse-riding and clay-pigeon shooting, as well as places of entertainment and a casino. In August and September every year the Lido is the venue for the International Film Festival (in the Palazzo del Cinema).

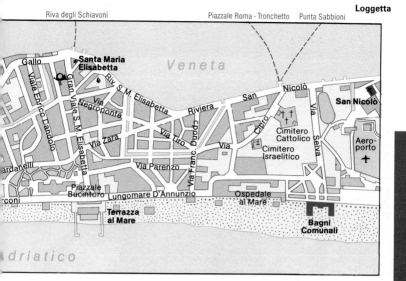

The main architectural feature is the massive *fin de siècle* hotels (the hotel Des Bains and its beach was the setting for Thomas Mann's novel "Death in Venice").

In the north part of the island there are villas, functional modern buildings and hotels, beach and residential districts.

Cars can be taken over by ferry, otherwise it is possible to get around on foot or by bus or horse-drawn cab.

Loggetta

K 5

The Loggetta at the foot of the Campanile in the Piazza di San Marco (see entries), a small marble loggia built by Sansovino between 1537 and 1540, was originally intended for the members of the Great Council so that they could assemble here whenever they wished, sheltered from rain and snow, before going into the sessions.

Location
Piazza di San
Marco/
Campanile

Quay
San Marco

However, as early as 1569 the elegant building, a work of art in itself, was downgraded to being the guardroom of the Doges Palace, which function it fulfilled until the end of the Republic in 1797.

In 1902 the Loggetta was crushed when the Campanile collapsed, but it was possible to rebuild it using the original stones and sculptures. Today it is a waiting-room for tourists wanting to ascent the Campanile by lift.

Sansovino's four bronze statues, "Pallas", "Apollo", "Mercury" and "Peace", between the twin columns are masterpieces.

59

Part of the beach on the Lido (see page 58)

★ Madonna dell'Orto (Santa Maria dell'Orto; church)   J 2

Location
Fondamenta della
Madonna dell'Orto

Quay
San Marcuola

The charming brick façade of this church (dating from 1462) which represents a blend of Gothic and Renaissance, contains a large number of outstanding sculptures. Some of these are ascribed to Jacobello dalle Masegne, one of the sculptors influenced by the northern Late Gothic style.

In the interior is the tomb of Tintoretto, whose real name was Jacopo Robusti and who was buried in 1594 in the chapel to the right of the Presbytery next to his son Domenico.

The church has several of his paintings: a "Last Judgment" (on the right of the choir), the "Worship of the Golden Calf" (on the left of the choir), "The Raising of Licinius by St Agnes" (fourth chapel on the left), the "Presentation of Mary in the Temple" (*c.* 1552) above the entrance to the Cappella di San Marco (in the right aisle). There are two noteworthy works by other artists: a "Madonna" (1480) by Giovanni Bellini (in the last chapel in the left aisle) and "St John the Baptist and four other Saints", a panel by Cima da Conegliano (1493; first altar on the right).

Merceria (shopping street)   K 4

Location
Merceria

Quay
Rialto/San Marco

Merceria is the main shopping street of Venice. It begins near the Rialto Bridge (see Ponte di Rialto) as a small square – in the centre is a statue commemorating the Italian dramatist Carlo Goldoni (see Famous People) – and winds its way to St Mark's Square (see Piazza di San Marco), emerging under the clock tower (see Torre dell'Orologio). The shops in this famous

Madonna dell'Orto Church on the Rio della Madonna dell'Orto

street offer a cosmopolitan range of goods, the emphasis being on textiles, particularly lace, leather goods (shoes and handbags) and glassware from Murano. The many small cafés and restaurants ("rosticceria", Tavola calda") offer many delicacies and local specialities.

In the Campo San Bartolomeo, at the beginning of the Merceria, businessmen still meet to conduct their transactions around the statue of Goldoni.

★★Monumento di Colleoni (Colleoni Monument)   L 4

The monument to Colleoni is a brilliant piece of work from the Venetian Renaissance. The model was made by Andrea Verocchil (1481–88) but it was cast in bronze by Alessandro Leopardi in 1496. The splendour of the plinth, with its marble reliefs, is taken up by the vigour of the equestrian figure, so that one balances the other in complete harmony. The figure itself bears no resemblance to the real Bartolomeo Colleoni (1400–75) but is an evocation of what the "condottier" should ideally look like – proud and conscious of his power.

Location
Campo SS
Giovanni
e Paolo

Quay
Rialto

Colleoni had commanded the land forces of the Republic, thus managing to amass a huge fortune. On his deathbed he bequeathed all his possessions to the State on the condition that a monument to his memory be erected "in front of San Marco". As the State, which hitherto had never authorised a public memorial, did not want to lose the money, instructions were given for the monument to be erected in front of the Scuolo Grande di San Marco (see entry), the confraternity house of San Marco, which stands next to the Church of Santi Giovanni e Paolo (see Zanipolo), since the dying man had failed to specify that his monument must be in front of the "Church" of San Marco!

Municipio (Town Hall) J/K 5

Location
Campo San Luca

The Town Hall consists of the Farsetti and Loredan palaces.

Quay
Rialto

Although the upper floors were altered in the 14th c., the ground floor of each palace has retained the 13th c. Byzantine floor plan.

★Murano (island) N/O 1 (A/B 7/8)

Quay
Murano (Line 12
from Fondamenta
Nuove)

Opening times
Glasshouses:
weekdays

Once a pleasure park where the rich nobility of Venice had their summer villas and where the first botanic garden in Italy was laid out, the face of Murano was transformed when the Republic transferred the glass workshops here in 1291. Officially a safety measure to counteract the fire risk in central Venice, the unofficial reason, and probably the more likely one, was that this was the most effective method of safeguarding what, until the 17th c., was Venice's best-kept secret – its method of glass-making. The glass-makers were well paid and enjoyed many privileges (they were allowed to carry swords and marry into the Venetian nobility) but were never allowed to leave the lagoon, thus retaining the knowledge of glass-making within Venice.

A Decree of the Council of Ten of 1454 runs thus: If a glass-blower takes his skill to another country to the detriment of the Republic he shall be ordered to return; should be refuse, his nearest relatives shall be thrown into prison so that his sense of family duty may induce him to return; should he persist in his disobedience secret measures shall be taken to eliminate him wherever he may be.''

Murano: glass-blowers

Murano: Glass Museum

The art of the glass-blowers can be admired in the workshops; each factory has its own shop for the sale of Murano glass – a rather expensive but much sought after souvenir.

The most important monument on the island is the Church of Santi Maria e Donato

Museo d'Arte Vetraria (Glass Museum)

The Glass Museum is housed in the Palazzo Giustinian which was built for the Bishop of Torcello in the 17th c. It contains one of the largest and most important collections of Venetian glass from the time of the Romans to the 20th c. – about 4000 items.

There are also displays of Bohemian and Moorish glass.

The most valuable piece is a 15th c. marriage bowl, dark blue and richly enamelled.

Most of the museum furnishings have been assembled from the churches on the island.

Opening times
Mon, Tues,
Thur–Sun.
10am–5pm

Admission charge

Santi Maria e Donato (church)

This splendid church was built between the 7th and 12th c. and combines Veneto-Byzantine and Early Romanesque features. Its façade with its superimposed arcades is justly famed.

Location
Campo San Donato

The splendours of the interior include:

The columns of Greek marble with Veneto-Byzantine capitals which separate the two aisles from the nave, and the 12th c. mosaic floor with its animal figures.

Church of Santi Maria e Donato on Murano

The painted wooden panel with the figure of St Donato (above the first altar on the left) dated 1310 is the earliest example of Venetian painting. It is said that the Venetian Crusaders brought the body of St Donato to Venice from Euboea and gave it to the basilica together with the remains of a dragon which Donato had killed; these relics can be seen on the wall behind the High Altar.

A Byzantine mosaic "Madonna at Prayer" (*c.* 1450).

Altar-piece "The Death of the Virgin Mary" on the wall of the left aisle (late 14th c.).

"The Madonna with Saints" in the entry to the Baptistery was painted by Lazzaro Bastiani in 1484.

A Sarcophagus from Altinum in the Baptistery was once used as a font.

San Pietro Martire (church)

Location
Fondamenta
Cavour

The 14th c. church (rebuilt in 1511 after a fire) contains several splendid Venetian paintings: "Madonna in Majesty with St Mark and the Doge Agostino Barbarigo" by Giovanni Bellini (1488; right aisle) and his "Assumption of the Virgin" which he painted between 1505 and 1513.

"St Jerome in the Wilderness" and "St Agatha in Prison" (left aisle) are by Paolo Veronese.

Museo Archeologico (Archaeological Museum)   K/L 5

Location
Piazza di San Marco
52

Quay
San Marco

Only some of the exhibits in this museum are in fact archaeological treasures, but the collection offers a unique opportunity to compare Classical archaeological finds with "modern" Renaissance art. Here the visitor can see the Classical sculptures that influenced the Renaissance artists of Venice.

Opening times
Daily 9am–7pm

Admission charge

The most important exhibits are:
Room 4: eleven Classical Greek korai dressed in chitons (5th c. B.C.).
Room 5: Statue of Apollo.
Room 6: Satyr and nymph embracing.
Room 7: Carved gem-stones.
Room 8: Running Odysseus (Hellenistic); Leda and the Swan; Roman busts.
Rooms 9–10: Busts from the Republic and Roman Empire.

Museo Archeologico

A Entrance to the Museum
B Entrance to the Library

Vestibolo
Piazzetta
Libreria Sansoviniana
Libreria Vecchia di San Marco
Courtyard
Entrance
Courtyard
Library
Curator's office

Piazza San Marco

FIRST FLOOR (PRIMO PIANO)
1 Corridor: Greek inscriptions
2 Coins
3 Copies of Greek sculptures
4 Greek sculptures
5 Roman copies of Greek sculptures
6 Dionysos and satyr; Grimani Altar, etc.
7 Hellenistic objets d'art
8 Galatian figures; Odysseus, etc.
9–10 Mainly Roman busts
11 Roman reliefs; Byzantine ivory-carvings
12–13 Roman art
14 Corridor: Roman art
15 Roman inscriptions
16 Unknown copies
17 Religious reliefs, etc.
18 Sculptures, statuettes, etc.
19 Objets d'art (ceramics, bronzes)
20 Assyrian reliefs; Egyptian mummies

Room 11: Byzantine ivory-carvings; St John the Evangelist and St Paul
(10th c.); St Theodore and St George.
Room 12: Reliefs of centaurs by T. Aspetti.
Room 20: Assyrian reliefs (8th–7th c. B.C.).

★Museo Civico Correr et Museo del Risorgimento   K 5
(Correr Museum and Risorgimento Museum)

The Correr Museum consists of an interesting collection illustrating the
history of Venice, and an important collection of paintings. The main
section covers both floors of the Procuratie and the entrance is in the
passage in the Ala Napoleonica (see entries).

The first floor is devoted to the historical collections (Rooms 1–14):
documents, etc. illustrating the architectural development of the city
(Room 1); paintings of scenes from the history of Venice, documents on the
development of the State coat of arms, the history of the Doges and the
political institutions (Rooms 3–10); State robes of the Doges, Procurators
and Senators, a large collection of Venetian coins; finally, documents, etc.
illustrating the history of Venetian shipping.

The second floor houses an art gallery with paintings from the 14th to the
17th c., including works by Lorenzo Veneziano, Jacobello del Fiore, Cosmè
Tura, Antonello da Messina, the Bellini brothers, Alvise Vivarini and
Carpaccio.

The Flemish masters are represented by Hugo van der Goes, Dirk Bouts,
Rogier van der Weiden and Pieter Brueghel.

Location
Procuratie Nuove
Piazza di San Marco
(entrance: Ala
Napoleonica)

Quay
San Marco

Opening times
Mon., Wed.–Sun.
10am–5pm

Admission charge

Museo del Risorgimento

The Museo del Risorgimento adjoins the Museo Civico Correr and contains
documents and illustrations of Venice's struggle against Austria, the 1848
Revolution led by Daniele Manin, and union with the kingdom of Sardinia-
Piedmont in 1866.

Museo di Icone dell'Instituto Ellenico (Icon Museum)   M 5

The former Scuolo di San Niccolò dei Greci (Palazzo Flangini), to the left of
the Church of San Giorgio dei Greci, houses a small but interesting icon
museum. Apart from the 14th–18th c. icôns it also contains richly embroidered liturgical robes and a collection of liturgical objects.

The Palazzo Flangini was built by Longhena in the 17th c.

Opening times: Mon., Wed.–Sat. 9am–1pm and 2–5pm, Sun. and public
holidays 9am–1pm.

Location
Salizzada dei
Greci

Quay
San Zaccaria

Admission charge

Museo di Storia Naturale

See Fondaco dei Turchi

Museo Storico Navale (Museum of Naval History)   N 6

The Museum of Naval History not only exhibits impressive booty brought
back from the numerous maritime wars of the Republic of San Marco, but

Location
Riva San Biagio

Palazzo Balbi

Palazzo Balbi – Site of the Central Administration of Venice

Quay
Arsenale

Opening times
Mon.–Sat.
9am–1pm

also uses models, mementoes and documents to give an account of ship-building and the types of vessels afloat in the period that Venice was a sea power, ending in 1797.

Also on display is a model of the legendary ship of state "Bucintoro". The Doge's sumptuous State galley was burnt out during the 1798 Jacobin Revolution.

Palazzo Balbi   G 5

Location
Rio Foscari

Quay
S. Tomà

This palace, situated on the broad mouth of the Rio Foscari, was built in 1582–90 to the plans of Alessandro Vittorio. The façade reveals characteristic features of Mannerism, the transitional architectural style between late Renaissance and early Baroque, expressed in the arrangement of double columns in the arcades, pierced gables and oval window openings. Since 1973 the Palace has been occupied by the central administration of Venice.

★Palazzo dei Camerlenghi (Palace of the Lords of the Exchequer)   K 4

Location
Campo
S. Giacomothe/
Ponte di Rialto
(entrance)

Quay
Rialto

Built across a corner, because of a bend in the Canal Grande, this marble palace near the Rialto bridge was once the seat of three most important Lords of the Venetian Exchequer and is a law court. The prestigious palazzo was built in 1525–28 by Guglielmo Grigo on the site of a former building which had burnt down in 1513. Its proportions are well balanced and it has attractive mezzo-reliefs, an interesting last testimony of Lombard Renaissance ornamentation. Its best side can be seen either from the Canal Grande or from the Ponte di Rialto (see entry).

Palazzo dei Camerlenghi

Palazzo Cavalli-Franchetti   H 6

Close to the Ponte dell'Accademia, the façade of the Palazzo Cavalli-Franchetti provides an excellent example of Late Gothic architecture. The building, which dates from 1565, was carefully restored in the 19th c. Of particular interest are the richly ornamented window frames. Part of the rear of the palace was enlarged in Neo-Gothic style. There is a small garden between the building and the Accademia bridge.

Location
Rio dell'Orso

Quay
Accademia

The staircase is considered one of the sights of Venice.

★Palazzo Contarini del Bovolo   J 5

The Palazzo Contarini del Bovolo is probably the only palace in Venice which has a courtyard that is more interesting than the façade overlooking the Canal (in this case the Rio dei Barcaroli). In the courtyard is the famous Scala di Bovolo, a spiral staircase built about 1500 by the architect Giovanni Candi, which gave the palace its nickname ("Bovolo" = spiral).

Location
Calle della Vida/
Rio dei Barcaroli

Quay
Rialto

★Palazzo Corner della Ca' Grande   H/J 6

The palace is one of the finest examples of High Renaissance architecture and today is the seat of the Prefettura (Prefecture).

This huge palace (hence its name "Ca' Grande" = big house) was built in the 16th c. by Jacopo Sansovino, the Italian master-builder and sculptor, for the Cornaro family.

Location
Canal Grande/
Fondamenta Corner
Zaguri (entrance)

Palazzo Corner della Regina

Palazzo Cavalli-Franchetti

Quay
Santa Maria del
Giglio

He gave the façade (overlooking the Canal Grande) Ionic columns on the first floor and Corinthian columns on the second.
    The interior was restored and modified in the 19th c.

★Palazzo Corner della Regina   J 3/4

Location
Calle Regina

Quay
San Staè

The outstanding feature of this huge Baroque palace, built in 1724 by Domenico Rossi, is the frieze of grotesque heads in the façade just above the water-level.
    The building was converted (unfortunately) from the Palazzo of Caterina Corner, Queen of Cyprus. The Corners, an old-established Venetian noble family, became so rich and powerful as a result of their sugar-cane plantation on Cyprus that the King of the island, James II, married the 18-year-old Caterina Corner in 1472. Eight months later the King died of poisoning. Caterina was forced to cede her kingdom to the Republic of Venice and in return was given Asolo as domain in exile and was allowed to spend the rest of her life (d. 1510) in her palace on the Canal Grande in a manner befitting her status. Thus Venice acquired Cyprus.
    Queen Caterina's palace today houses the archives of the Biennale. The main façade overlooks the Canal Grande.

★Palazzo Corner-Spinelli   H 5

Location
Rio Ca' Corner/
Canal Grande

Quay
Sant'Angelo

As well as the twin-arched windows and the curved balconies, the particularly remarkable feature of this palace is its upper storey with its rich yet well-ordered ornamentation. The interior was designed in 1542 by Sanmicheli.

The main façade overlooks the Canal Grande.

★Palazzo Dolfin-Manin

K 4

Another large palace with an impressive façade, the Palazzo Dolfin-Manin was built between 1538 and 1560 by Sansovino. It was the residence of the 120th and last Doge, Ludovico Manin, during his time in office (1789–1797). Today it houses the Banca d'Italia.

Manin's elevation to the office of Doge, when he declared himself in such a state of trepidation that he hardly knew what he was doing, was followed on May 12th 1797 with his being obliged to declare the dissolution of the 1000-year-old Republic of St Mark when, with the words "It will not be needed any more", he handed over his insignia of office. He had to make his country residence, Campo Formio in Friuli, available for the negotiations that led to Napoleon's handing the "city on the water" over to Austria as a "consolation prize".

Location
Riva del Ferro/
Canal Grande

Quay
Rialto

★★Palazzo Ducale (Doges' Palace)

L 5

The Doges' Palace was the centre of government of the Republic and the residence of the Doge (see Introduction, Government of the Venetian City State under the Doges). Apparently a square building, it actually consists of only three wings: the wing along the Rio Palazzo, the main façade on the Molo (71m/233ft) and the west façade (75m/246ft) overlooking the Piazzetta. The fourth wing is formed by the Basilica di San Marco (Basilica of St Mark, see entry) which the palace has adjoined since 1438.
   The first palace of the Doges, a wretched gloomy wooden fortress with massive defensive towers, was built in 814. It was surrounded by the lagoon on the south side and by canals on the other sides. The castle was entered by a drawbridge on the north side. After frequent destruction by fire and subsequent rebuilding, the castle was converted in the 12th c. into a palace in the Byzantine style. Fragments of the foundations are all that remain of these early Palazzi.
   The present palace was built mainly in the 14th c., and the façade overlooking the Piazzetta mostly dates from the first half of the 15th c.
   The courtyard and the main interior were reconstructed in the Renaissance style after a fire in 1483. The first architect was Filippo Calendario; the master-builders of the Bon family used his plans to complete the two main façades in the Gothic-Venetian style in the years leading up to 1462. The palace was completed in 1550.

The astonishing exterior of the palace is often referred to as a symbol of the "city on piles". The fragile filigree of the Loggia with its 71 columns and almost Oriental tracery stands on the 36 short columns of the ground floor. Above is a massive block of marble with six large windows and a richly ornamented Gothic balcony. It is faced with white and pink marble in a diamond pattern. On top is a cornice of merlons and spires. The amazing tension created by this combination caused André Suarès to exclaim "So much graceful strength on such fragile foundations!"

Location
Piazzetta

Quay
Riva Degli
Schiavoni

Opening times
daily 9am–7pm

Admission charge

Exterior

South front
The south façade with its two lower Gothic windows is the oldest part of the exterior. The beautiful capitals symbolising Vice and Virtue (14th–15th c.) are worthy of note. The large balcony window dates from 1404 and the figure on the gable, Venice as "Justice", from 1579.

West front
The west façade is mostly 15th c. It copies the style of the south front (balcony windows, gable statue). The capitals here – allegorical themes, foliage – are also noteworthy.

West façade of the Palazzo Ducale on the Piazzetta

In earlier times sentences of death used to be proclaimed from a position between the ninth and tenth columns of the Loggia (the only ones made of red marble).

Porta della Carta
The Porta della Carta (the main entrance) was created as the link between the Doges' Palace and the Basilica by the brothers Giovanni and Bartolomeo Bon (1438–32). Together with the Ca' d'Oro (see entry) it is considered a perfect example of Venetian Gothic.

The door is surrounded by a framework of ornamentation and allegorical figures; above is Doge Francesco Foscari kneeling before the Lion of St Mark (symbolising the attitude of the Venetians towards their State – the individual bows to the power of the State). The present sculpture is a 19th c. copy of the original which was destroyed in 1797.

The Porta della Carta (Paper Gate) is thought to be so named from the petitioners who used to wait here for the members of the Council and the Government in order to hand over their petitions and requests. The laws of the Republic were also proclaimed in front of the gate, at the corner of the Basilica di San Marco, on the stump of a column used for that purpose.

Foscari Arch
The Porta della Carta leads into the courtyard through the Foscari Arch, a Gothic porch richly ornamented with columns, niches and turrets, and already displaying elements of the Renaissance style, especially in the statues of Adam and Eve by the sculptor Antonio Rizzo (these are copies, the original stand in the Quarantia Criminal on the second floor).

Courtyard
The courtyard, redesigned by Antonio Rizzo after a fire in 1483, is a Renaissance masterpiece. After Rizzo fled, having been accused of embezzlement, the upper part of the main façade of the courtyard was completed by his successors; west and south façades, refaced early in the 17th c.

Scala dei Giganti: the Giants' Staircase, designed by Rizzo

Cortile dei Senatori
To the left of the main courtyard is the Cortile dei Senatori with a Late
Renaissance front and beautiful marble ornamentation. This is where the
Senators used to gather before receptions. The little chapel next to it was
the Doge's private chapel (now closed).

Scala dei Giganti
The Staircase of the Giants, also designed and begun by Rizzo, adjoins the
Foscari Arch and leads up to the State apartments on the first floor. Its top
landing is where the Doges were crowned – and, in the case of Doge Marino
Fliero, beheaded. The Coronation procedure was for the newly elected
Doge to take his oath, whereupon the youngest member of the Great
Council would hand him the white "corno" (Doge's cap) and the senior
member would place it on his head.
   The staircase owes its name to the two larger-than-life-size figures of
Mars and Neptune symbolising Venice's power on land and sea. They are
the work of Jacopo Sansovino (1567).

The Palazzo Ducale is now a museum but, unlike the general run of
museums, the paintings on display here were created especially to decorate the Doges' Palace, not added later. Visitors follow a marked itinerary.

Interior of
the Palace

Museo dell' Opera
The Museo dell' Opera on the ground floor of the Doge's Palace exhibits
original items of the decoration of the building which have had to be
replaced by copies.

Scala d'Oro
The main and side staircases of the Scala d'Oro lead from the Loggia on the
first floor to the second floor and thence to the offices and reception rooms
on the third floor. In earlier times only members of the Council and the
Doge's guests of honour were allowed to use them.

Sala del Senato in the Palazzo Ducale

This impressive staircase, which gets its name from its rich gold orna-mentation, was probably begun by Sansovino in 1538 and completed by Scarpagnino about 1550.

Atrio Quadrato

This anteroom contains a remarkable ceiling-painting by Tintoretto of the Doge Girolamo Priuli (1561–1564) appearing before Venice and with justice presenting him with the Sword and the Scales in the presence of his Patron Saint and Peace. All the wall-paintings are also based on the theme of Venice.

Sala delle Quattro Porte

The Hall of the Four Doors was decorated in accordance with Palladio's designs. The ceiling and the frescoes are from the Studio of Tintoretto. The wall-painting "Doge Antonio Grimani before the Faith" was begun by Titian about 1600 and completed by another artist.

Sala dell'Anticollegio

This beautiful, richly decorated hall was mainly used as a waiting-room for foreign delegations. The paintings are by Tintoretto, Paolo Veronese and Jacopo Bassano.

Tintoretto's four paintings are based on mythological events and give a new interpretation to the history of Venice: "Minerva dismissing Mars" (victory of wisdom over force); "Vulcan and Cyclops forging weapons for Venice"; Mercury and the Three Graces" (Venice's commercial activities are recompensed by beauty); "The Marriage of Bacchus and Ariadne" (Venice's marriage with the sea).

Napoleon had Veronese's "Rape of Europa" taken to Paris, but it was later returned together with other art treasures.

Bassano's painting depicts the scene from the Old Testament of the return of Jacob with his family.

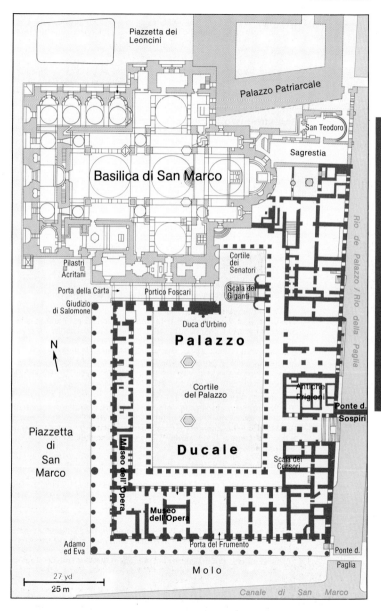

Piazzetta dei Leoncini

Palazzo Patriarcale

San Teodoro

Sagrestia

Basilica di San Marco

Pilastri Acritani

Porta della Carta

Portico Foscari

Cortile dei Senatori

Scala dei Giganti

Giudizio di Salomone

Duca d'Urbino

N

Palazzo

Cortile del Palazzo

Antiche Prigioni

Ponte d. Sospiri

Piazzetta di San Marco

Museo dell'Opera

Ducale

Scala dei Censori

Museo dell'Opera

Adamo ed Eva

Porta del Frumento

Ponte d.

Paglia

Rio de Palazzo / Rio della Paglia

M o l o

Canale di San Marco

27 yd

25 m

Sala del Collegio

This hall, probably the most beautiful room in the whole palace, is where the "Collegio" (the Cabinet of the Government) met under the chairmanship of the Doge, and where the Republic received its most important visitors.

What most impresses the visitor are the harmonious proportions of the room and the unity of decoration and furnishings. The large wall-painting of 1578 above the Doge's throne is by Veronese and depicts Doge Sebastiano Venici offering thanks to Christ for the victory of the Venetians over the Turks in the Battle of Lepanto.

The ceiling by Francesco Bello is the finest in the palace and has a wonderful series of paintings by Veronese (c. 1577). As everywhere else in the palace, these paintings take as their subjects the ideals that formed the basis of the State of Venice: "Mars and Neptune" (power on land and sea), "Faith" (piety), "Justice and Peace". The borders depict the virtues of the State: dog (fidelity), horn of plenty (industry), crane (vigilance), spider's web (diligence), eagle (self-control), sceptre (magnanimity), dove (peaceableness), lamb (meekness).

The wall-paintings are by Tintoretto or his pupils. Near the entrance is Tintoretto's "Doge Andrea Gritti kneeling before the Virgin".

Sala del Senato

The Senate met twice a week in this hall. Consisting of the Doge, members of the College and some 60 members of the Great Council, the Senate laid down policy guidelines and made decisions on peace and war.

Most of the paintings are by Jacopo Palmer the Younger and reiterate the theme of the glorification of Venice.

Private chapel (not always accessible)

The Doge's private chapel has a fine "Madonna" by Sansovino.

Sala del Consiglio dei Dieci

The Council of Ten, which sat here, was the secret State court. It was in charge of the secret police and controlled every aspect of public and private life. There was no appeal against a judgment given by the Ten.

A harmonious blend of wood panelling, gilding and paintings, including Veronese's "Jupiter hurling his thunderbolts against the Vices", a copy of the original in the Louvre and an allusion to the work of the Council of Ten, and "Juno offering the Ducal Crown to Venice".

Sala della Bussola

The wooden compass in the right-hand corner gave this room its name (there are two doors hidden behind it). In this room those summoned to appear before the Council of Ten waited to be examined. Next to the door is a Bocca di Leone ("lion's mouth"), into which secret denunciations could be dropped.

Sala dei Tre Capi

This room belonged to the three Chief Magistrates elected from the Council of Ten to form the Court of Inquisition which dealt with acts of high treason and espionage and kept the nobles under surveillance. Anyone brought before them was as good as dead.

Sale dei Inquisitori

The inquisitors, who met here, were the examining magistrates whose task was to interrogate offenders, if necessary with the aid of red-hot pincers, the rack and the thumbscrew.

The room was originally covered entirely in leather. The picture in the middle of the ceiling is Tintoretto's "Return of the Prodigal Son".

Armoury

The next rooms once housed the armoury of the Republic and nowadays have over 2200 weapons and suits of armour (mostly 15th–16th c.) on display.

Andito del Maggior Consiglio
This vestibule with its gilded ceiling beams is where the members of the Great Council waited before the sessions and during the breaks.

Sala della Quarantia Civil Vecchia
The civil court which sat here consisted of a body of 40 (hence Quarantia) lawyers. The framed picture of the Virgin dates from the 15th c. and the large wall-paintings from the 17th c.

Sala del Guariento
This room contains the undamaged fragments of the large fresco painted in 1365 by the artist Guariento (hence the room's name) for the Sala del Maggior Consiglio (Hall of the Great Council) which was burnt out by the great fire of 1577.

Sala del Maggior Consiglio
This Hall of the Great Council, the seat of the Lower House of the Venetian Parliament, is impressive not so much because of its size (54m/177ft × 25m/82ft) but because of its harmonious proportions in relation to its size. It was made so large not simply in order to be imposing but also on purely practical grounds, since when the Council was in session it had to accommodate up to 1800 citizens entitled to vote. It therefore had rows of seats in the middle, along the two long walls and against the west wall; the short east wall with the tribune was reserved for the Doge and the highest officials. The hall was built between 1340 and 1355.

The greatest artists of their time took part in painting the room. From Padua came Guariento, whose painting above the Doge's throne was destroyed by fire (see Sale del Guariento) and replaced in 1588 by Tintoretto's "Paradise" which is still in place. The fire of 1577 also destroyed the paintings by Gentile da Fabriano, Pisanello, Giovanni Bellini, Carpaccio and Titian.

Reconstruction (in its original form) was entrusted to Antonio da Ponte, who built the Ponte di Rialto (see entry). Tintoretto and Veronese did the paintings, assisted by Palma the Younger and Francesco Bassano.

Tintoretto's "Paradise" (22m/71ft × 7m/23ft) ranks as the largest oil-painting in the world and its great mass of figures make it difficult for the viewer to take in the picture as a whole. Close inspection shows that Tintoretto ranged the figures in accordance with their rank, grouping them in circles and segments of circles with Christ and his Mother in the centre at the top.

Another masterpiece is the ceiling with panels painted by Veronese – "Venezia". Venice surrounded by gods and crowned by Victory.

Other masterly ceiling-paintings are "Doge Ponte paying homage to Venice" by Tintoretto, and "Venice welcoming the conquered Nations around her Throne" by Palma the Younger.

The wall canvasses depict scenes from Venetian history. The frieze, just under the ceiling, of the first 76 Doges is the work of Domenico Tintoretto and his assistants; the portrait of Doge Marino Faliero, who was beheaded, has been painted out in black (see Introduction, Government of the Venetian City State).

The Sala del Maggior Consiglio was where all the decisions which made the Republic a World Power were discussed. It was also where the Republic was declared to have been dissolved in 1797.

The tour now continues in the Doge's apartments on the second floor of the east wing.

Sala dello Scrutinio
The Voting Hall was where public elections, including the election of the Doge, were prepared and carried out. The paintings, including "The Conquest of Zara" by Tintoretto (right wall) depict Venetian battles on land and sea.

Palazzo Ducale

Ponte dei Sospiri

Magnificent oriel window, Palazzo Ducale

Sala dello Scudo
The maps, copies of originals of about 1540, document Venetian rule.

Sala Griman
Special features are the ceiling, with its gold ornamentation on a blue ground, and the frieze of allegorical subjects (after 1504).

Sala Erizzo
An interesting 16th c. ceiling and 15th–17th c. marble and stucco chimneypiece.

Sala degli Stucchi
The stucco on the vaulted ceiling dates from the 17th c.; the stucco and painted inserts on the walls were added in the 18th c.

Small staircase of the Doges
Above the door is a fresco by Titian, "St Christopher" (1523–24), the only painting by this artist in the Doge's Palace to have survived.

Sale dei Filosofi
This vestibule gave access to the Doge's apartments.

Pinacoteca
The rooms at the back of the Doge's apartments contain a small picture gallery with works by Giovanni Bellini, Hieronymus Bosch, Boccaccio Boccaccini, Antonello de Saliba, Tiepolo and Tintoretto.

Ponte dei Sospiri
The Bridge of Sighs is an enclosed arched bridge over the Rio di Palazzo joining the first floor of the Doge's Palace with the first floor of the prison.
    Completed by Antonio da Ponte in 1603, today it is one of the main tourist attractions of Venice, although less because of its attractive Baroque shape

than because of its name and significance; it was over this bridge that prisoners were taken before the judges, and the sentences given by Venetian judges were as hard and unmerciful as the laws of the Republic.

Prigioni
Until about 1750 there were no escapes from the State prison and even Casanova only managed to get out by an extremely hazardous route.

Especially feared were the piombi ("lead chambers"), the low narrow cells right under the lead roof which were like furnaces in summer.

The cells once had wooden walls, ceilings and floors, but now only the stone walls and iron-barred windows are left.

★Palazzo Grassi   H 5

The three-storeyed building, of which the relatively plain façade decoration incorporates both Baroque and Classical features, was constructed in the mid-18th c. from plans by the architect Giorgio Massari. He decided on a ground plan, unusual in Venice, which involved building around an extended rectangular courtyard.

Location
Canal Grande/
Campo San
Samuele

Quay
San Samuele

The Palazzo was built for the Grassi family who lived there until the beginning of the 20th c. Then it was bought by the civic authorities and used as a museum and congress centre. When the Fiat Motor Company acquired the palace extensive restoration was undertaken in 1985, with the idea of recreating the original structure. However, this intention was not strictly carried out. For example – even if it is technically improved – the roofing over of the inner courtyard, carried out in 1951, has meant that the usefulness of the palazzo has been maintained. With the aim of converting the building into a cultural centre of the first rank the artistic direction was entrusted to the internationally well-known Swede Pontus Hulten. He

Palazzo Grassi

organised an opening exhibition in the summer of 1986 which proved very successful. In future this stately building will house a comprehensive summer exhibition and a smaller one in winter, as well as creating a home for theatrical and musical events.

The palace faces the Canal Grande.

★Palazzo Grimani   J 5

Location
Canal Grande/
Rio di San Luca

Quay
Rialto

This palace was built in 1556, where the Rio di San Luca flows into the Canal Grande, for the Procurator.Girolamo Grimani by Michele Sanmicheli from Verona. The towering façade with its massive window arches was completed in the following year by Giangicomo, who also worked on the second storey. The palazzo was completed in 1575 by Giovanni Rusconi. Alessandro Vittorio was responsible for the ornamentation of the doorway.

Today it houses the Appeal Court of Venice.

The main façade overlooks the Canal Grande.

★Palazzo Loredan dell'Ambasciatore   G 6

Location
Calle dei Cerchieri

Quay
Ca' Rezzonico

This is a marvellous Gothic palace with two especially interesting seahorses created by a follower of Vittoria on the façade.

In the 18th c. the palace was the residence of the Ambassador of the Holy Roman Empire, hence its popular name "Palazzo dell'Ambasciatore (Ambassador's Palace).

The main façade overlooks the Canal Grande.

Palazzo Mocenigo-Nero   H 5

Location
Calle Mocenigo

Quay
San Samuele

Built in the 17th c. this is one of a group of palaces which all belonged to the aristocratic Mocenigo family. Seven members of the family held the office of Doge of Venice between 1414 and 1778 and thus left their mark on Venetian history. Adjoining the Palazzo Moncenigo-Nero is a double palace where Byron lived in 1818 and 1819. The oldest Moncenigo palace is the Casa Vecchia (1579) in Late Renaissance style.

★Palazzo Pesaro (Gallery of Modern Art and Museum of Oriental Art)   J 3

Location
Fondamenta
Mocenigo/
Canal Grande

Quay
San Staè

The palace was built between 1652 and 1710 by the masters of Venetian Late Baroque, Baldassare Longhena and Antonio Gaspari. Sansovino's Library (see Libreria Vecchia) in the Piazzetta (see entry) was used as a model for the splendid façade. After the death of the last Pesaro in 1830 there was a succession of owners, until the City of Venice acquired the palace in 1902.

**Galleria d'Arte
Moderna**

Today the lavishly designed interior houses the Galleria d'Arte Moderna (Gallery of Modern Art). The gallery was founded at the end of the last century after the first biennial in 1897 and has one of the most important collections of modern art in Italy.

Among its most interesting exhibits are works by the Munich Realist Franz von Lenbach, the Munich Secessionists Franze von Lenbach and Franz von Stuck, Auguste Rodin and Marc Chagall.

The gallery is open Tues.–Sun. 10am–5pm

**Museo d'Arte
Orientale**

On the third floor is the Museo d'Arte Orientale (Museum of Oriental Art). It has an outstanding collection of Far Eastern objects d'art, e.g. Chinese vases, Japanese paintings, Indian sculpture. The museum is open Tues.–Sun. 9am–2pm. The main façade overlooks the Canal Grande.

Palazzi Corner della Regina and Pesaro (on the right)

Palazzo Querini-Stampalia (library and museum)   **L 5**

The attractive palace houses the Querini-Stampalia art gallery and library which were bequeathed to the city, together with the palace, in 1868.
   The art gallery is closed at the present time for restoration work.

Biblioteca Querini-Stampalia
The library is on the first floor and contains 1,100,000 Venetian volumes and 300 manuscripts.

Pinacoteca Querini-Stampalia
The collection of 14th–18th c. Venetian paintings is on the second floor. The pictures are still arranged according to the wishes of the founder of the collection Count Giovanni Querini-Stampalia. There are works by Donato Venaziano (Room 2), Sebastiano Bombelli (Room 3), Palma the Younger (Room 4), Andrea Schiavone (Room 5), Pietro Liberi, Matteo dei Pitocchi (Rooms 6–7), Giovanni Bellini, Lorenzo di Credi (Room 8), Palmer the Elder (Room 9), Pietro Longhi (Rooms 11–13), Alesandro Longhi, Giambattista Tiepolo (Room 18), and Bernard Strozzi (Room 19).
   Apart from the paintings the Venetian 18th c. furniture is of special interest.

Location
Campiello Querini-Stampalia

Quay
Rialto

Admission charge

★Palazzo Rezzonico e Museo del Settecento Veneziano   **G 5**
(Museum of 18th c. Venice)

The massive building was begun in 1660 by Baldassare Longhena, the greatest Baroque architect in Venice, and was completed nearly 100 years later (1750) by Giorgio Massari for the noble Rezzonico family.

In 1687 one member of this family bought himself the patent of nobility, as Pope Clement XIII.

Location
Rio di Santa Barnabà/
Canal Grande

79

Museo del Settecento Veneziano

Quay
Ca'Rezzonio

Opening times
daily 10am–5pm

Admission charge

The museum's collection, in keeping with the design and decoration of the palace, gives a fascinating glimpse of life in Venice in the Rococo period. There are some 40 display rooms: silk wall-coverings, Flemish tapestries, cabinets and chests of drawers (including some splendid pieces by Andrea Brustolon), the Chinoiserie and lacquered furniture so popular at that time, Venetian porcelain and pottery, bronzes and puppets.

Of special interest are the original 18th c. Venetian costumes and a meticulously reconstructed 18th c. chemist's shop, and also a theatre (third floor).

★Palazzo Vendramin-Calergi   H 3

Location
Calle Colombia/
Canal Grande

Quay
San Marcuolo

This palace is a perfect example of Venetian Renaissance architecture and towards the end of the last century many of its elements were copied throughout Europe.

The palace was built between 1480 and 1504 by Mauro Coducci. At first it belonged to the Loredan family, then in the 16th c. to the Calergi family, and finally in the 18th c. it came into the hands of the Vendramin family. Richard Wagner died here in 1883. In winter the casino is housed here.

Palazzo Zenobio   F 5

Location
Rio Dei Carmini

Quay
Ca'Rezzonico

This palace in the Dorsoduro district was built by the architect Antonio Gaspari between 1680 and 1685.

The façade is Baroque, but in its plain structure the building shows elements of the Classical style.

Palazzo Vendramin-Calergi

Pescheria (fish market) J 4

Dating only from 1907 the market hall near the Rialto Bridge was built by
Domenico Rupolo and Cesare Laurenti in Gothic style on the site of the
traditional fish market, its skilful architecture (especially the ingenious
capitals on the columns) and the activity among the various stalls make it
an attractive feature of Venice. The building was constructed according to a
centuries old method on over 18,000 larch wood piles.
  The fish market is open on weekdays from 5–11am.

Location
Canal Grande/Ponte
di Rialto (access)

Quay
Rialto

★★Piazza di San Marco (St Mark's Square) K 5

St Mark's Square, "la Piazza" for short, is Venice on parade, the point
around which Venetian life revolves. Considered one of the finest squares
in the world, it conveys a perfect impression of the city's former greatness
since round it are grouped the buildings on which were centred the civic
and religious life of the Republic. Surrounded on three sides by the arcades
of public buildings – the Procuratie Vecchie (north), the Ala Napoleonica
(west) and the Procuratie Nuove (south) – the integrated beauty of this
unique square is rounded off by the domes and arches of the Basilica di San
Marco (east) and the slender, soaring Campanile (see entries).
  The square, paved with trachyte, is completely open without a single
monument or roadway to detract from the unbroken architectural unity.
The only traffic is the visitors (and the famous pigeons). The square
becomes narrower as it approaches the Ala Napoleonica, which gives it
considerable greater depth: over an average length of 175m/574ft it nar-
rows from 82m/269ft at the Basilica to 56.6m/185½ft at the other end.
  Originally the Piazza was full of fruit trees with a canal running across it.
The completion of the Basilica and the enlargement of the Palazzo Ducale
(see entry) also saw a start made on landscaping the square. First came the
Campanile (begun in 912 and completed in the 12th c., followed in 1204 by
the Procuratie Vecchie; the fruit trees disappeared, the canal was filled in
and in 1267 the square covered with paving slabs. 1583 saw the building of
the Procuratie Nuove. Having been paved with marble in 1735 (the big
white squares originally marked the sites where the individual craftsmen's
guilds were allowed to erect their market stalls), the square finally acquired
its present aspect with the building of the Napoleonic Wing.
  Until the fall of the Republic the Piazza di San Marco was a "market-
place". Today it is a place to see and be seen, to stroll in or to sit and listen to
the bands playing at the square's world-famous cafés.
  The pigeons of San Marco are also part of the picture. Fed at the public
charge (although there are no set feeding-times), they are the acknow-
ledged protégés of the Venetians. Whatever their origins – whether de-
scended from the birds brought to the lagoon in the 5th c. by the early
Venetians on their flight from Attila, or from those set free by the Doges
each Palm Sunday, or even from the carrier pigeons that brought the news
of the capture of Constantinople in 1204 – they are an institution.

Quay
San Marco

Piazzetta K/L 5

This charming square is where Venice really receives its visitors. It is open
to the sea, with the two columns on the Molo (Colonne di Marco e Teodoro),
bordered on the right by the Palazzo Ducale (Doge's Palace), on the left by
the Libreria Vecchia (library), backed by the Campanile on one side and the
projecting Basilica di San Marco (Basilica of St Mark) on the other with, in
the background, the Torre dell'Orologio (Clock Tower) and the Procuratie
(see entries). The Piazzetta opens into the Palazzo di San Marco (see entry)

Location
San Marco

St Theodore on his column in the Piazzetta

of which it is almost a part. It acquired its present shape with the building of the library. In the early Middle Ages a broad canal ran alongside the Doge's Palace up to the Basilica di San Marco.

Ponte dell'Accademia (Academy Bridge)   H 6

For centuries the only bridge over the Canal Grande was the Ponte di Rialto (see entry), then in 1854 Austria, the occupying power since 1815 when Venice became part of the Habsburg Kingdom of Lombardy-Veneto, decided to erect a second footbridge and the Ponte dell'Accademia, a small iron bridge, was built. In 1932 the iron bridge was demolished and replaced by a wooden bridge. Looked upon as a temporary measure, it was to be replaced by a stone bridge, but this was never built. At present the Ponte dell'Accademia is not accessible because it is unsafe.

Quay
Accademia

★Ponte di Rialto (Rialto Bridge)   K 4

For a long time the Ponte di Rialto was the only footbridge over the Canal Grande; the Ponte dell'Accademia (see entry) was not built until 1854 and the Ponte Scalzi near the station is 20th c. It gets its name from "Rivus Altus" (high bank) which was the name given to the earliest settlement on the island. The first wooden bridge built on this spot as early as 1180, later to be replaced by a drawbridge which collapsed in 1444 under the weight of a crowd of people who had gathered to watch a boat procession. Almost 150 years later, in 1588, the Venetians embarked upon the venture of building a stone bridge. Designed by Antonio de Ponte, the bridge is supported by 6000 piles on each side and its single arch is 22m/72ft in span and 7.5m/24ft high.

Location
Ponte di Rialto

Quay
Rialto

◀ *Piazza di San Marco*

Ponte di Rialto

Procuratie (Procurators' Office)   K 5

Location
Piazza di San Marco

Quay
San Marco

The north and south sides of the Piazza di San Marco (see entry) are bordered by the Procuratie, the former offices of the Procurators of San Marco, the chief officials of the Republic. Today the buildings house, amongst other things, the Museo Correr together with the Museo del Risorgimento and the Museo Archeologico (see entries).

There was a Procurator as early as the 10th c. After the Doge, he was the most important man in the State and was answerable to no one, not even the Great Council. The Procurator was the "Custodian of St Mark", of the wealth that accumulated in the coffers of the Basilica di San Marco (see entry) as a result of public and private gifts, bequests and regular income. The sums in question were enormous, since a donation was always made to St Mark as a matter of course in thanksgiving for a successful and profitable enterprise.

It was with this huge fortune that the State financed all that it owned, the construction of San Marco and every one of its welfare institutions: hospitals, alms distribution, hostels for the homeless, homes for the aged and orphanages – institutions that guaranteed even the poorest the means of subsistence.

It soon became impossible for one person to shoulder alone the burden of the work that came to be involved in administering the public purse; in the 13th c. there were four Procurators, in 1319 six and in 1442 nine.

Procuratie Vecchie
(Old Procurators'
Offices) (north
side of the Piazza)

In 1204 there was a two-storey building on the present-day site of the Procuratie Vecchie. The present three-storey building dates from between 1480 and 1517; the architect was Mauro Codocci and the building work was completed by Bartolomeo Bon. It is a very fine example of Venetian Early Renaissance architecture and has arcades along the length of its façade (150m/164yd) – 50 on the ground floor and 100 on each of the upper floors.

Procuratie Vecchie in the Piazza di San Marco

When even the enlarged Procuratie Vecchie became too small the building of the Procuratie Nuove was begun in 1582 on the south side of the Piazza di San Marco. The architect Vincenzo Scamozzi used Sansovino's library as a model, adding another storey and topping it with a cornice (instead of a balustrade). Baldassare Longhena completed the building in 1640 in accordance with Scamozzi's original plans.

Procuratie Nuove (New Procurator's Offices) (south side of the Piazza)

Today the former official residence of the Procurators houses the Museo Civico Correr, where the magnificent official robes of the Procurators can be seen, the Museo del Risorgimento and the Museo Archeologico (see entries).

Between 1805 and 1814 Napoleon lived in the Procuratie Nuove whenever, in his capacity as "King of Italy", he visited Venice, his second Italian seat of residence after Milan.

Raccolta Peggy Guggenheim (Peggy Guggenheim Collection)

See Ca' Venier dei Leoni

Il Redentore (church)

See La Giudecca, Il Redentore

Rialto Bridge

See Ponte di Rialto

San Bartolomeo (church)   K 4

Location
Campo San
Bartolomeo

Quay
Rialto

This was the church of the German merchants in Venice for which Albrecht Dürer painted his famous "Feast of the Rosary" (1506), later acquired by Emperor Rudolf II and taken to Prague where it is still to be found.

In the choir of the church on the former organ wings are the paintings of four saints by Sebastiano del Piombo (c. 1485–1547). The altar-piece on the High Altar, "The Martyrdom of St Bartholomew" by Palma the Younger, is also of interest.

San Francesco del Deserto (island)

Quay
San Francesco del
Deserto (from Riva
degli Schiavoni)

According to legend St Francis of Assisi rested on this tiny island on his way back from the Holy Land (1220). The little church dating from 1228, surrounded by cypresses, has a charming atmosphere. After a visit it is customary to give the monks a small donation. Visitors welcome Mon.–Fri. 9–11am and 3–5pm.

San Francesco della Vigna (church)   H 4

Location
Campo San
Francesco
della Vigna

Quay
San Zaccaria

Opening times
Daily 9–11am,
3–5pm

Work on this large church was begun by Sansovino in 1534, It was not completed until 40 years later when Andrea Palladio assumed the main responsibility for the façade (1568–72).

The church contains some interesting paintings: in the south transept is an important panel-painting, "The Enthroned Madonna" (c. 1450) by Antonio da Negroponte. The Cappella Santa (access from the north transept) has a "Madonna and Saints" by Giovanni Bellini (1507), one of his later works. In the Sacristy is a triptych by Antonio Vivarini (15th c.) and in the fifth chapel on the left a "Madonna" by Paolo Veronese (1551).

Also interesting is a 15th c. series of sculptures by Pietro Lombardo in the Cappella Giustiniani (to the left of the High Altar).

San Giacomo dell'Orio (church)   N 4

Location
Campo San
Giacomo
dell'Orio

Quay
San Staè

The church and its Romanesque Campanile date back in their present form to the 16th c. The Presbytery, which has a richly carved ceiling, was not added until later. The altar-piece, "Sacred Conversation" (1546), by Lorenzo Lotto is especially interesting. The Old Sacristy contains works by Palma Giovane.

The New Sacristy is situated outside the building and has fine ceiling paintings by Paolo Veronese.

★San Giobbe (church)   F 2

Location
Campo San Giobbe

Quay
Ferrovia
(railway station)

The Church of San Giobbe is the first example of Tuscan Renaissance architecture in Venice. It was built by Antonio Gambello (from 1450) who began the church in the Late Gothic style (the Campanile is of that period) and Pietro Lombardo (from 1471).

Especially interesting are Paris Bordone's "St Peter" dating from the 16th c. (fourth side-altar on the right), and the fine tomb-slab of Doge Cristoforo Moro, the church's founder, dated 1470, which is in front of the High Altar. In the Sacristy is a triptych by Antonio Vivarini (c. 1445) which can be seen on request.

The way to the church is along the Canale di Cannaregio and then left at the bridge, the Ponte del Tre Archi.

San Giorgio Maggiore (island)   L/M 6/7

The American Henry James once wrote of the island that it has "a success beyond all reason". The island owes its beauty mainly to its position and to the genius of the Venetian architects. The first church was built in 790, and two hundred years later the Benedictine monastery was added. Both buildings were destroyed by an earthquake. The monastery was rebuilt and in the 16th c. San Giorgio Maggiore was built on the site of the old church. After the Second World War the buildings on the island became increasingly dilapidated until finally the Italian industrialist Vittorio Cini established the Giorgio Cini Foundation in memory of his son Giorgio. This foundation financed restoration of the dilapidated and decaying buildings and built an International Centre of Art and Culture with 30 auditoria, a cinema, an open-air theatre and a naval college.

In 1980 the Western Heads of State met on San Giorgio Maggiore for the famous Venice Economic Summit Conference.

Quay
San Giorgio

★San Giorgio Maggiore (church)

The first church of San Giorgio Maggiore was built here about 790. The present building dates from 1566. It was begun by Andrea Palladio but was not completed until 1610, thirty years after his death, by Scamozzi. The present bell tower dates from the 18th c. It is well worth taking the lift to the top as from the platform there is a marvellous panoramic view of the city and the lagoon (entrance to the left of the monastic choir).

Quay
San Giorgio

Opening times
Campanile:
9am–noon and
2.30–6pm

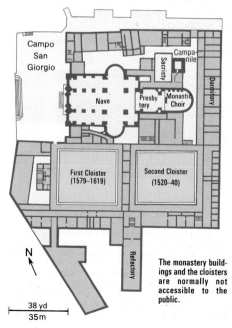

San Giorgio Maggiore

Of special interest within the church:

S aisle
On the second altar a splendid wooden Crucifix (late 15th c.)
On the third altar a painting from the school of Tintoretto, "The Martyrdom of St Cosmas and St Damian"

N aisle
On the second altar a marble sculpture by Girolamo Campagna (1595)

S transept
Altarpiece from Tintoretto's studio, "The Coronation of the Virgin" (1594)

N transept
"The Martyrdom of St Stephen" by Tintoretto

Presbytery
At the front two bronze candelsticks dated 1598. "The Shower of Manna" and "The Last Supper" (1594) by Tintoretto

Monastic Choir
Splendid Baroque stalls

High Altar
Bronze sculpture by Girolamo Campagna (late 16th c.)

The monastery buildings and the cloisters are normally not accessible to the public.

87

Island and Church of San Giorgio Maggiore

Admission charge   The most important painting in the church is "The Shower of Manna" by Tintoretto in the Presbytery. The High Altar is the work of Girolamo Campagna, a pupil of Sansovino (late 16th c.).

San Giovanni in Bragora (church)   M 5

Location
Campo Bandiera
e Moro

Quay
Arsenale

This church is one of the oldest in Venice and was founded as early as the 7th c. It was built in its present Late-Gothic style in 1475 and the Presbytery was added in 1485–94.

Inside are three masterpieces of early Venetian painting. In the apse of the choir is Cima da Conegliano's "Baptism of Christ" (1494) in a marble frame, one of the master's finest works. In the left choir chapel is a triptych by Bartolomeo Vivarini, "The Madonna Enthroned between St John the Baptist and St Andrew" (1478). In the first side-chapel on the left (next to the entrance) is a "Resurrection" by Alvise Vivarini (1498), an early Renaissance work.

Over the entrance is an interesting work by Palma Giovane, "Christ before Caiaphas" (1600).

San Giovanni Crisostomo (church)   K 4

Quay
Rialto

This domed Renaissance-style church, in the form of a Greek cross, is one of the masterpieces of Mauro Coducci who built it between 1479 and 1504 on the foundations of an earlier church. It is dedicated to St Chrysostom.

Of interest in the interior is a late work by Giovanni Bellini, "St Jerome, St Christopher and St Augustine" (1513; first side chapel on the right) and, over the High Altar, "Madonna and Saints" (including St Chrysostom; 1509–11) by Sebastiano del Piombo.

Also of interest is the marble bas-relief (1500–02) by Tullio Lombardo on the second altar on the left.

San Marcuola (officially: Santi Ermagora e Fortunato; church)   H 3

The Church of San Marcuola was built between 1728 and 1736 by the architect Giorgio Massari, but the façade overlooking the Canal Grande was never completed.

   The most important works of art are "The Last Supper" by Tintoretto (1547; Presbytery, left-hand wall), a popular interpretation of Leonardo da Vinci's Milan picture (1495–97), and an old copy of his "Washing of the Feet" (opposite). It is also worth noting that the altars are richly decorated not with paintings but with sculptures.

Location
Campo San Marcuola

Quay
San Marcuola

San Michele (island)   M/N 1/2

San Michele is the cemetery island of Venice. The present cemetery was laid out in the 19th c. Since it is on an island, the cemetery's capacity is limited and most Venetians can only count on having a resting-place there for 12 years, after which the remains are reinterred communally and burial-places are reused.

   Of the monastery which used to be here there remains the 15th c. cloister, together with the attractive Renaissance Church of San Michele, built by Mauro Coducci (1469–78).

   The hexagonal Cappella Emiliana added by Guglielmo Bergamasco in 1530 is also worth seeing.

Quay
San Michele (Line 12 from Fondamenta Nuove, or line 5 from Riva degli Schiavoni)

San Moisè (church)   K 5/6

Art connoisseurs find the Baroque façade of the church (built by Alessandro Tremignon in 1668) too rich and over-ornate. But the people of Venice love their "San Moisè" with its typical Venetian bell-tower.

Location
Calle Largo 22 Marzo

San Marcuola

Quay
San Marco

Worth seeing in the interior are a "Pieta" dating from 1732 (interior wall of the façade), a bronze relief of the Deposition (designed by Roccatagliata brothers in 1633; Sacristy altar), and the Baroque sculpture on the High Altar depicting Moses receiving the Tablets on Mount Sinai (by the Austrian Meyring).

San Nicolò (church)

Location
Lido

Quay
San Nicolò

This church dates back to 1044 but was reconstructed in the Baroque style in the 17th c. and has an unfinished façade.

It was once thought that this church contained the remains of St Nicholas that Venetian sailors had stolen from the cathedral of the town on Myra (which belonged at that time to the Byzantine Empire) on the south coast of Asia Minor (opposite Rhodes). Some time after this had been celebrated and the monastery and church had been founded, the Venetians discovered that the people of Bari in Apulia had made away with the remains of the "real" St Nicholas.

The cloisters and paintings by both Palma the Elder and Younger are of interest.

San Pietro di Castello (church)   Q 5

Location
Campo San Pietro

Quay
Giardini

On the island of San Pietro di Castello, at the eastern edge of the city and on the site of Olivolo, one of the first settlements in the lagoon, this church was built to serve Venice as its first cathedral.

According to legend, in the 7th c. Bishop Magnus of Altinum had a vision of St Peter who ordered him to build a church "where he found sheep and goats grazing". From 775 onwards the Church of San Pietro was the episcopal church and from 1451 to 1807 it was the church of the Patriarchs of Venice. This function was not taken over by the Basilica di San Marco (see entry) until after the fall of the Republic.

The present church was built in the 17th c. Its façade is thought to be based on a design by Palladio. The Campanile was designed by Mauro Coducci (1482–88) in the Early Renaissance style. The original tower roof collapsed in 1670.

Of interest are the Baroque High Altar by Baldassare Longhena (1649) and the so-called "Cattedra di San Pietro", the marble throne supposed to have been used by St Peter in Antioch.

San Polo (officially San Paolo; church)   H 4

Location
Campo San Polo

Quay
San Silvestro

The original Later Gothic church, founded in the 9th c. was reconstructed and drastically altered in the 19th c.; the Campanile (14th c.) has survived unaltered.

Of interest inside is "The Last Supper" which Tintoretto painted in 1568–69. This is his second version of the theme; another one dating from 1547 is in the Church of San Marcuola (see entry) while a third version, which he painted much later, can be seen in San Giorgio Maggiore (see entry). Also of interested in San Polo are the bronze statue near the High Altar by Alessandro Vittoria and G. B. Tiepolo's painting "Madonna with St John of Nepomuk".

San Salvatore (church)   K 5

The 7th c. church was reconstructed between 1507 and 1534 by Tullio
Lombardo and Sansovino, and given its present Baroque façade by Giuseppe Sardi between 1663 and 1700. There is reason to suppose that its
creators intended that San Salvatore should rival the Basilica di San Marco
(see entry) in its size and splendour, but it has only three domes as compared with five of San Marco.

Location
Calle Mazzini

Quay
Rialto

The interior has retained its Renaissance style and houses several important works of art. The baldachins give the impression of great
spaciousness.

The most interesting of the monuments is the splendid memorial to
Doge Francesco Venier, designed by Sansovino (1556–61; past the second
altar on the left).

The outstanding paintings are the two works by Titian: "The Annunciation" (third altar on the right, with a marble frame by Sansovino) and "The
Transfiguration of Christ" (on the High Altar). Another interesting painting
by Giovanni Bellini is on the wall of the left choir chapel.

★San Sabastiano (church)   F 6

The Renaissance Church of San Sabastiano was built between 1505 and
1546. This is where Paolo Veronese who decorated the interior almost
single-handed is buried (on the left of the choir). Numbered among his
most important works is "The Coronation of the Virgin" and on the ceiling
in the Sacristy are the four panels of the Evangelists which made his
reputation (entrance under the organ). On the ceiling of the nave are his
scenes from the Life of Esther: "Esther taken before Ahasuerus", Esther
crowned Queen", "The Triumph of Mordecai". The splendid frames of the
ceiling-paintings are also interesting.

Location
Campo San
Sabastiano

Quay
Ca'Rezzonico

The wall-paintings (also in the nave) are by Paolo Veronese and his
brother Benedetto. The organ-case was also designed and painted by
Paolo Veronese.

In 1558 in the Nun's Choir he painted the frescoes "St Sebastian before
Diocletian" and "The Martyrdom of St Sebastian".

On the High Altar is one of the artist's later works "Madonna in Majesty
with SS Sebastian, Peter, Catherine and Francis".

San Silvestro   J 4

Although the present church was only built in 1836–43, the foundation
goes back to the 9th c. The Classical façade was completed in 1909. Over
the first side altar on the right can be seen the monumental painting "The
Baptism of Christ" (1580) by Jacopo Tintoretto. In contrast to his picture on
the same biblical subject in the Scuolo di San Rocco (see entry), this
painting is confined to a personal meeting between John the Baptist and
Christ, who is illuminated by the dove of the Holy Spirit.

Location
Campo di San
Silvestro

Quay
San Silvestro

San Simeone Piccolo   F 4

Opposite the rail station stands the Church of San Simeone Piccolo, its
dome covered in a green patina. The church was built in 1718–38 by
Giovanni Scalfurotto on the site of the medieval church of SS Simeone e
Guida. The Late Baroque architecture is modelled on the Pantheon in
Rome, but also has Classical Renaissance features. A broad flight of steps
leads up to the Palladian pillared portico which gives access to the actual
church. Inside can be seen a "Pieta" by J. Palma Giovane.

Location
Fondamenta di San
Simeone Piccolo

Quay
Piazzale Roma

San Simeone Piccolo

San Staè (officially: Sant'Eustachio; church)   H 3

Location
Campo San Staè/
Canal Grande

Quay
San Staè

The church, which was built in 1678 by Giovanni Grassi, is in the shape of a Greek cross. The façade on the Grand Canal was added thirty years later in 1709 by the master-builder Domenico Rossi. The funds came from Alvise Mocenigo II who was Doge from 1700–09, and who is buried in the church.

The interior is decorated with early 18th c. works, including G. B. Piazetta's "The Martyrdom of St James the Great", Sebastiano Ricci's "The Freeing of St Peter", "The Torment of St Bartholomew" by G. B. Tiepolo and "The Crucifixion of St Andrew" by G. A. Pellegrini.

San Trovaso (officially L Santi Gervasio e Protasio; church)   G 6

Location
Campo San
Trovaso

Quay
Accademia

This church is in fact dedicated to SS Gervase and Protase but their names were finally abbreviated to Trovaso. The interior is simple but it has several paintings by well-known artists: Tintoretto's "The Last Supper" (left transept) and "The Temptation of St Antony" (left choir chapel), and "St Chrysogonus" by Michele Giambono (right choir chapel).

The most important works of art in the church are the marble altar reliefs (right transept) by an unknown artist. They are thought to date from about 1470.

San Zaccaria (church)   L/M 5

Location
Campo San
Zaccaria

This church was probably founded in the 9th c. The present church was built between 1444 and 1500 by the two great master builders Antonio Gambello and Mauro Coducci. The huge façade is an astounding example

San Staè, Baroque-style church

of the transition from Gothic to Early Renaissance architecture. It is the most important work of the Venetian Renaissance before it lost its individuality with Sansovino and adopted the forms of the mainland. The Campanile is still Byzantine, the choir still Gothic and the nave is in the style of the early Renaissance.

Quay
San Zaccaria

Of especial interest are Giovanni Bellini's "Enthroned Madonna with Saints" dating from 1505 (second side-altar on the left) and Andrea del Castagno's frescoes (1452) in the Cappella di San Tarasio.

San Zaccaria was considered the rowdiest of all the convents in the rowdy city of 18th c. Venice. The riotous parties held in the convent and the love-affairs indulged in by the nuns were the talk of the town. This was because most of San Zaccaria's nuns were the daughters of noble families sent there against their will to save the expense of dowries. Cheated out of their lives they found their own way of avenging themselves.

Santa Maria della Fava (church)   K 4

This 18th c. church has a single nave lined with reliefs and statues by Giuseppe Bernardi, the teacher of Antonio Canova. It also contains an early work by G. B. Tiepolo, "Anna, Joachim and Mary" (1732; first side chapel on the right) and a masterpiece by G. B. Piazzetta, "St Filippo Neri begging for the Poor" (1725–27; second side altar on the left).

Location
Calle della Fava

Quay
Rialto

★Santa Maria Formosa (church)   L 4/5

Mauro Coducci built this church in 1492 on the foundations of an older, probably 11th c. church (the façade overlooking the Campo and the Baroque bell-tower were added in the 17th c.). The result was an extremely successful merging of a basic Byzantine shape and Venetian Renaissance

Location
Campo Santa Maria Formosa

93

Santa Maria Formosa and market-place

Quay
Rialto

architecture, and an interior which, with its slender columns, little cupolas and barrel-vaults, gives the impression of being Byzantine yet is smothered with marvellous Renaissance ornamentation.

The most interesting works of art are Bartolomeo Vivarini's altar-piece "Madonna of Mercy (1473) and a "St Barbara" (early 16th c; Palma Vecchio) in the chapel to the right of the high altar. Every morning the square around the church, the Campo Santa Maria Formosa, is the scene of a fruit market as it has been for centuries. The church stands in the centre of the square which is bordered on two sides by canals.

Until the fall of the Republic it was traditional for the Doge to visit the church every year at Candlemas. This commemorated a day in 944 when a number of girls on their way to church were abducted by Slavs from Dalmatia. They were rescued by the Scuola dei Casselleri (Guild of Makers of Marriage Coffers), who had their oratory in the church. As their reward the Doge was asked to make an annual visit to the church at Candlemas. "But what shall I do if it rains?" asked the Doge. "We shall give you a hat". "And what shall I do if I am thirsty?", "We shall give you wine". From then on every year at Candlemas the Doge was given a straw hat and a flagon of wine at the Church of Santa Maria Formosa. One of the hats can be seen in the Museo Correr (see entry).

★Santa Maria dei Miracoli (church)   K/L 4

Location
Calle delle Erbe

Quay
Rialto

Santa Maria dei Miracoli is a masterpiece of Early Renaissance architecture by Pietro Lombardo (1481–89) built to enshrine a miraculous picture of the Virgin. Instead of decorating the exterior with sculpture Lombardo used cleverly matched coloured marble arranged to form rosettes, circles, octagons and crosses on the façade. The interior is embellished in the same way, with the golden domed ceiling achieving a much greater effect above the grey and coral marble walls as a result. Steps lead from the nave to the chancel which is partitioned off by an exquisite Early Renaissance balustrade decorated with figures. This interior is one of the most beautiful in all Venice.

★Santa Maria della Salute (church)　　　　　　　　　J 6

This Baroque domed church was built to commemorate the plague which in 1630 claimed over 40,000 victims in Venice alone. Baldassare Longhena began the work in 1631 on foundations of over one million wooden piles. It was not completed until 1687, five years after his death. Longhena's design was only accepted by the Senate because it "would make a grand impression without costing too much".

Location
Fondamenta Salute

Quay
Salute

Santa Maria della Salute (The Church of our Lady) depicts Mary as "Ruler of the Sea" (Capitana del Mar); the statue of the Virgin on the top of the dome carries the staff of command of a Venetian Admiral of the Fleet.

The broad flight of steps leading up to the church and its two huge domes not only gives it an astounding breadth but also enhances the whole cityscape. Seen from the sea (the true "view of Venice") Santa Maria della Salute perfectly offsets the Basilica di San Marco, the Palazzo Ducale and the Campanile (see entries). In the last few decades it has been severely damaged by pollution, as has almost the whole city, but in recent years has been restored with money provided by the French Save Venice Fund.

The interior is rather austere. Of the 120 sculptures the group on the High Altar by Juste Le Court is probably the most important: the Madonna complying with the fervent request of Venezia and driving out the plague. The faithful commemorate the end of the plague and the founding of the church by holding a solemn service and procession every year on November 21st, The Feast of the Salvation.

The paintings in The Great Sacristy are also interesting: Tintoretto's "The Wedding at Cana" (long wall) and Titian's ceiling-paintings "Cain and Abel", "The Sacrifice of Abraham" and "David and Goliath" (1542–44).

To the left of the church is the Seminario Patriarcale which houses the Manfredinian Picture Gallery (see Seminario e Pinacoteca Manfrediniana).

Santa Maria Zobenigo (officially: Santa Maria del Giglio; church)　　J 6

The church was founded in the 9th c. by the Zubanico family, hence its name, but it is usually called Santa Maria del Giglio. The interior was restored in 1660 and the Baroque façade was added in 1678–83 by Giuseppe Sardi on the orders of Antonio Barbaro who, as a quid pro quo, ensured his own immortality by having a stone statue of himself placed above the main portal with, underneath, some of his ancestors. The lower plinths are decorated with reliefs showing panoramas of the cities in which Antonio Barbaro had served: Padua, Candia in Crete, and Zara (left), Rome, Corfu and Spalato (right).

Location
Campo Santa Maria del Giglio

Quay
San Marco

The Presbytery contains an early work by Tintoretto, "The Four Evangelists" (1552–57).

Santi Apostoli (church)　　　　　　　　　　　　　　　K 4

This 14th c. church (reconstructed in the 18th c.) is really only of interest because of the superb Corner family chapel (on the right of the nave), attributed to Mauro Coducci in the late 15th c. It is one of the finest examples of Venetian Renaissance architecture, originally intended as the burial-place of the Queen of Cyprus. The richly carved columns and the delicate cupola achieve an astonishing harmony.

Location
Campo dei Santi Apostoli

Quay
Ca' d'Oro

Santa Maria della Salute (see page 95)

Giambattista Tiepolo's altar-piece, "The Communion of St Lucy" (1746–48) is radiantly beautiful.

Santi Giovanni e Paolo

See Zanipolo

Santo Stefano (church)   H/J 5

Location
Campo Morosoni

Quay
Accademia

The Late Gothic church at the top end of the Campo Morosoni dates from 1374. The perilously crooked Campanile, the gables on the façade, the choir and the splendid wooden vault in the nave were added 150 years later.

Two important Venetians are buried in the simple interior. In the nave is the tomb-slab of Doge Francesco Morosoni who recaptured the Peloponnese for Venice, but at the same time blew up the Parthenon on the Acropolis which was used by the Turks to store their gunpowder.

The composer Giovanni Gabriele (1557–1612) is buried in front of the first altar on the left. He was organist at San Marco (see Basilica di San Marco) and a pioneer of Early Baroque music. Santo Stefano also contains several valuable paintings by Venetian artists, including several by Tintoretto: "The Last Supper", "Christ Washing the Disciples' Feet" and in the Sacristy "The Agony in the Garden". In the first altar on the right is "The Birth of the Virgin" by Nicolò Bambini.

Apart from the paintings the Late Gothic choir-stalls in the Presbytery and the fragments of a choir screen (both 1488) are very interesting.

The fine monastery cloister (entrance at the east end of the north aisle) is also worth seeing.

Scuola dei Carmini (confraternity house of the Carmelites) F 5

This Scuola formerly served one of the six most important confraternities
of Venice. The Scuole were not schools but meeting-places and houses of
prayer for religious fraternities where Venetian citizens banded together.
They were organised either according to country of origin or according to
occupation, had specific religious or charitable aims and above all provided mutual assistance and charitable benefits. They were often very rich,
and this is demonstrated by their splendid confraternity houses.

The Scuola dei Carmini belonged to a lay confraternity of Carmelites
who, nevertheless, were able to commission such important artists as
Giambattista Tiepolo and Nicolò Bambini to decorate their house for them.
In the hall on the upper floor Tiepolo created nine ceiling-paintings between 1739 and 1744, including his most mature work "Mary handing St
Simon the Scapular of the Carmelites". He was paid only 400 sequins for
this fresco.

The other paintings, including those by Bambini, all dating from the
18th c. are also of interest.

Location
Campo Santa
Margherita

Quay
Ca' Rezzonico

Scuola Grande di San Marco (confraternity house of San Marco) L 4

The Scuola Grande di San Marco, adjoining the Church of Santi Giovanni e
Paolo (see Zanipolo), served the rich confraternity of goldsmiths and silk-
merchants. Today it is a municipal hospital. The lower part of the building
was begun about 1490 by Pietro Lombardo; his son Tullio did the reliefs
and the two lions. Mauro Coducci finally completed the building in about
1500 by adding the upper part with its stepped round gables crowned with
figures.

Location
Campo SS
Giovanni
e Paolo

Quay
Rialto

Scuola Grande di San Marco

97

Scuola Grande di San Rocco

Not open to the public

Although not as clear-cut as Santa Maria dei Miracoli nor as forceful as San Zaccaria (see entries), the splendid façade is, nevertheless, one of the outstanding examples of Venetian Renaissance architecture. The "trompe-l'œil" effects on the ground floor, the fluid arches and the sculpture on the gables combine to fine effect.

The sculpture in the lunette of the doorway "St Mark with the Brethren of the Scuola" is attributed to Bartolomeo Bon who also worked on the Porta della Carta in the Doge's Palace (see Palazzo Ducale).

★Scuola Grande di San Rocco (confraternity house of San Rocco) G 4/5

Location
Campo San Rocco

Quay
San Tomà

This impressive white marble building was constructed between 1515 and 1560 to a design by Bartolomeo Bon. The Scuola has become world-famous because of its series of paintings by the great 16th c. artist Tintoretto.

Opening times
Daily 9am–1pm,
Sat. Sun. also
3.30–6.30pm

Ground floor
Eight large paintings by the Master with scenes from the Life of the Virgin, including "The Annunciation", "The Flight into Egypt" and "The Massacre of the Innocents".

Admission charge

Upper floor
The large hall has ceiling- and wall-paintings executed by Tintoretto between 1575 and 1581.

The works in the Committee Room (Sala dell'Albergo) date back to 1564 and 1576, and include "The Glorification of St Roch", "Christ before Pilate", the "Ecce Homo" and "The Crucifixion".

Scuola di San Giorgio degli Schiavoni M5
(confraternity house of St George of the Dalmatians)

Location
Calle dei Furlani

Quay
San Zaccaria

Opening times
Tues.–Sat.
9.30am–12.30pm,
3–6.30pm, Sun. and
public holidays
9.30am–12.30pm

Admission charge

This was the Scuola of the Dalmatian merchants, the "Schiavoni" (Slavs). Between 1502 and 1508 Vittore Carpaccio decorated its walls with the cycle of paintings which still survive complete and which rank as his most important work alongside his pictures in the Galleria dell'Accademia, the Museo Correr and the Ca' d'Oro (see entries).

There are no captions to the pictures. Those on the left wall are "St George killing the Dragon" and "The Triumph of St George".

Left and right of the altar: "St George baptising the heathen King and Queen" and "St Tryphon exorcising the Daughter of the Emperor Gordianus".

Right wall: "The Agony in the Garden", "The Calling of St Matthew", "St Jerome leading his Lion into a Monastery", "The Funeral of St Jerome", and "St Jerome in his Study".

Seminario e Pinacoteca Manfrediniana J/K 6
(seminary building and art gallery)

Location
Fondamenta Salute

Quay
Salute

Opening times
By appointment
only

The Seminario Patriarcale to the left of the Church of Santa Maria della Salute (see entry) houses the Pinacoteca Manfrediniana. The Seminario and the church were both designed by Longhena (1669).

The art collection of Marquis Federico Manfredini of Florence contains terracotta busts by Alessandro Vittoria (1515–1608), paintings by Antonio Vivarini (15th c.), Cima da Conegliano, Konrad Laib and Filippini Lippi; a major work by Antonio Canova (1757–1822; a bust of Gian Matteo Amadei) and a ceiling-painting in the library, "Glory of the Sciences" (c. 1720 by Sebastiano Ricci).

★Teatro La Fenice (La Fenice theatre)   J 5

The Teatro La Fenice is the opera-house of Venice. Built between 1790 and 1792, it was rebuilt in its original Neo-Classical style in 1836 after a fire.

Its interior is richly decorated with gold, pink and white stucco, carvings and gilding. Rossini, Bellini and Verdi composed operas specially for this splendid theatre which thus saw the first perfomances of Verdi's "Ernani" (1844), "Rigoletto" (1851), "La Traviata" (1853) and "Simon Boccanegra" (1857). It also staged the première of Benjamin Britten's "The Turn of the Screw".

Incidentally, the rapturous reception for Verdi and the incessant chants of "Viva Verdi" were not simply on grounds of artistic merit. VERDI spelt out the clarion call of Italian opposition to Austrian rule and stood for Vittorio Emanuele Re d'Italia (Victor Emanuel, King of Italy).

Today La Fenice is the most important opera house in Italy after La Scala, Milan.

Location
Calle San Fantin

Quay
San Marco

Season
November–July
Tel: 78 65 11
Fax: 5 22 17 68

★Torcello (island)

Torcello is the real precursor of Venice. It was founded on the island as early as the 7th c. and in the 12th c. was a flourishing commercial town with palaces and churches, shipyards and docks, its own nobility, its own laws and a large population. The large town has vanished leaving only two churches and a handful of houses dotted over this large island.

The cathedral serves as the main proof of its former importance.

Quay
Torcello (Line 12 from Fondamenta Nuove)

Santa Maria Assunta (cathedral)

Dedicated in 639 to Santa Maria Assunta, the cathedral is probably the best example of the Venetian-Byzantine style of architecture. Reconstructed in 834 and 1008, the portico and the two lateral apses were added in the 9th c.; the main fabric of the building dates from the 11th c.

The cathedral contains some beautiful mosaics.

Opening times
daily 10am–12.30pm, 2–6pm

Admission charge

Right side-chapels
The oldest mosaics are in the chapel to the right of the High Altar. The angels carrying a medallion with the Lamb of God are still strongly marked by Byzantine influence (11th c.; vaulting of the apse). The Fathers of the Church, Gregory, Martin, Ambrose and Augustine were added later, as was the "Christ in Majesty between two Archangels" (concha of the apse).

Interior of the cathedral

Main apse
The mosaics in the main apse date from the 12th c.: the Virgin and Child above a frieze of the Twelve Apostles standing among flowers, all on a gold ground.

West side
The west wall of the cathedral is covered by the tiers of a Byzantine mosaic of the Last Judgment dating from the late 12th or early 13th c.

Top tier: Christ at the shattered gates of Limbo.
Second tier: Christ as Judge of the World.

Third tier: Christ enthroned with the Archangels Michael and Gabriel, and Adam and Eve (kneeling); also angels sounding the trumpets heralding the Last Judgment (at the sides).

On either side of the door: the Blessed (clothed), the Damned (naked).

The rood-screen
The upper part is decorated with pictures representing the Virgin and the Twelve Apostles, while the lower part has reliefs with representations of peacocks and lions.

Other points of interest

Santa Maria Assunta: Virgin and Child . . .   . . . Christ in Majesty (12th c.)

The High Altar
This dates from the 7th c. and was restored in the early 20th c. Also of interest are the iconostasis (15th c.), the mosaic floor (11th c.) and the pulpit (assembled in the 13th c. from earlier fragments).

Santa Fosca (church)

The small Church of Saint Fosca adjoining the cathedral is centrally planned and purely Byzantine. Dating from the 11th c. it has a portico on five sides and its interior is of unusually harmonious proportions.

Torre dell'Orologio (clock tower)   K 5

Location
Piazza di San Marco

Quay
San Marco

Closed at present for restoration

The clock tower was designed and built (1496–99) by Mauro Coducci, probably to finish off the Procuratie Vecchie (see entry). It is typical of Venetian Renaissance architecture.

The top storey with the mosaic of gold stars strewn over a blue background and the Lion of St Mark were added in 1755 by Giorgio Massari.

The two bronze Mori Moors on the terrace who strike the bell to mark the hours were cast by Paolo Ranieri (1494–97). Visitors can climb to the roof of the clock tower to get a closer view of these two figures.

The magnificent great clock (from which the tower gets its name) was also made by Ranieri and his son. It shows the hours, phases of the moon and the signs of the zodiac. Above the clock-face is a gilded Madonna. During Ascension Week and at Epiphany the Three Kings are conducted by an angel past the Madonna at each hour.

Below the clock tower is the passage leading to the shopping street of Merceria (see entry).

★Zanipolo (officially: Santi Giovanni et Paolo; Dominican church)   L 4

Next to the Franciscan Church of I Frari (see entry), the church of the Mendicant Order of Dominicans, the Zanipolo, is the prime example of Late Gothic ecclesiastical architecture in Venice. The vast brick structure, dating from 1333 to 1390, is sometimes justifiably referred to as the "Pantheon of the Doges". Eleven Doges were buried here in the 15th and 16th centuries. Many of their tombs were designed by Pietro Lombardo, the architect of the Church of Santa Maria dei Miracoli (see entry), and his equally famous son Tullio.

Location
Campo SS
Giovanni
et Paolo

Tombs
Of especial interest are the wall-tomb of Doge Andreas Vendramin (d. 1478) on the left side of the sanctuary, the work (1492–95) of Tullio Lombardo, and on the right of the entrance the tomb of Doge Pietro Mocenigo, which Pietro Lombardo created in 1481. Other notable people who are buried in the church are Marco Corner (d. 1368), Michele Morosine (d. 1382), Leonardo Loredan (d. 1521), Jacopo Cavalli (d. 1384), the Venier family (15th–16th c.), Pasquale Malipiero (d. 1462), Bertucci Valier (d. 1708), Tommaso Mocenigo (d. 1423), Niccolò Marcello (d. 1474), Giovanni Mocenigo (d. 1485) and Alvise I (d. 1577.

Interior of
the church

Cappella del Rosario
Formerly decorated with works by Tintoretto and Palma the Younger which were all destroyed in the fire of 1867, the ceiling has paintings by Veronese:

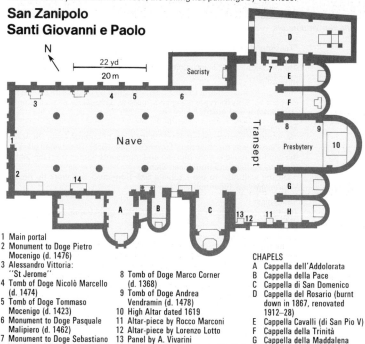

San Zanipolo
Santi Giovanni e Paolo

1 Main portal
2 Monument to Doge Pietro Mocenigo (d. 1476)
3 Alessandro Vittoria: "St Jerome"
4 Tomb of Doge Nicolò Marcello (d. 1474)
5 Tomb of Doge Tommaso Mocenigo (d. 1423)
6 Monument to Doge Pasquale Malipiero (d. 1462)
7 Monument to Doge Sebastiano Venier (d. 1578)
8 Tomb of Doge Marco Corner (d. 1368)
9 Tomb of Doge Andrea Vendramin (d. 1478)
10 High Altar dated 1619
11 Altar-piece by Rocco Marconi
12 Altar-piece by Lorenzo Lotto
13 Panel by A. Vivarini
14 Altar with panel by Giovanni Bellini

CHAPELS
A Cappella dell'Addolorata
B Cappella della Pace
C Cappella di San Domenico
D Cappella del Rosario (burnt down in 1867, renovated 1912–28)
E Cappella Cavalli (di San Pio V)
F Cappella della Trinità
G Cappella della Maddalena
H Cappella del Crocifisso

Zanipolo

Cappella dell' Addolorata

Cappella del Rosario

"The Adoration of the Magi" (in the Presbytery), "The Assumption of the Virgin (at the front of the chapel), "The Adoration of the Shepherds", "The Annunciation" and "The Nativity" (on the wall by the entrance).

High Altar
The High Altar is thought to have been designed by Baldassare Longhena in about 1619. Its Baroque design was used as a model for altars in southern Germany and Austria.

South transept
"St Antonius Pieruzzi giving Alms" is the work of Lorenzo Lotto (St Antonius Pieruzzi was Archbishop of Florence (1480–1556). The stained glass in the window above is from Murano and represents figures from the Bible, the Early Fathers and Dominican Saints.

On the wall next to the Cappella San Domenico is a work by Alvise Vivarini entitled "Bearing the Cross".

South aisle
The early Renaissance Polyptych, still in its original frame, is by Giovanni Bellini (*c.* 1465).

Palazzo Rezzenico on the Canal Grande ▶

Practical Information

Airport

Venice's airport is Marco Polo International Airport near Tessara, 13km/8 miles north-east of the city. Transport to and from Venice is by bus or motor launch (see Getting to Venice). Nicelli Airport in San Nicolò di Lido can only be used by small aircraft.

Airport information

Tel. 66 11 11

Airlines

Alitalia
Campo San Moisè, San Marco 1757;
tel. 5 26 61 11
Aeroporto Marco Polo;
tel. 2 60 63 11

British Airways
Riva degli Schiavoni, San Marco 4158;
tel. 5 28 20 26

TWA (general sales)
San Marco 1475;
tel. 5 20 32 19 and 5 20 32 20

Banks

Opening times

Open: Mon.–Fri. 8.30am–1.30 or 2pm and 3–4pm.

S.V.E.T. (Soc. Viaggi e Turismo),
Piazza San Marco, San Marco 145a
Open Mon.–Sat. 9am–12.30pm, Sun., public holidays
9am–12.30pm, 2.30–6.30pm

American Express
Salizzada San Moisè, San Marco 1471
Open Mon.–Sat. 8am–8pm

American Service Bank
San Marco 1336

Banca d'America e d'Italia
Via XXII Marzo 2216/7

Banca d'Italia
San Marco 4799

Banca Nazionale del Lavorno (Bureau de change)
Rio Terrà A. Foscarini 877/d (near the Accademia)

Banca Nazionale delle Comunicazioni
Stazione San Lucia (railway station)
Open also on Sun. and public holidays

Biennale

See Events

Cafés

The first person in Italy who spoke or wrote about coffee was Francesco Morosini, the Doge's ambassador at Constantinople 1582–85. "In Turkey they drink a black water which is produced from a seed called samen, and which, so they say, has the ability of keeping people awake." Anyone strolling through Venice will now find in all the larger squares a stand-up café or a patisserie with enticing pastries, delightful cream cakes, *biscottini*, *pasticcini* and other delicacies, which can be enjoyed at any time of the day as snacks to accompany a cup of coffee.

Established meeting-places of Venice are the historic cafés in St Mark's Square: the Lavena, the Florian beneath the Baroque arches of the Procuratie Nuove and the Quadri, immediately opposite. The situation of these last two cafés had political overtones in the 19th century when the Venetian patriots, Manin and Tommaseo, preferred the Florian, while Austrian officers favoured the Quadri.

The Café Florian was opened in 1720. This, the oldest coffee house of Venice, has been called by this title ever since it relinquished the original name of "Venezia triofante" in order to adopt the name of its owner, Floriano Francesconi. The interior of the café, which is furnished in various styles (including Chinese, Turkish and "Senate" rooms), is a protected building and has long been significant in world literature with such celebrated patrons as Goethe, Honoré de Balzac, Marcel Proust, Thomas Mann, Ernest Hemingway and Mark Twain.

★Florian

Café Florian – 19th c. meeting place of patrons of Venice

Café Quadri – with an atmosphere of the past

★Quadri

The atmosphere of the past can also be felt in the Quadri, although this café is fifty years younger than the Florian. It is famous for its cakes and pastries and its cooking and is named after its original proprietor, Giorgio Quadri, a Levantine from Corfu, who in his day could prepare the best "coffee in the Turkish manner". The resident orchestra has Viennese music in its repertoire.

★Lavena

The Café Lavena, founded in 1750 and carefully restored in 1990 has the old-fashioned furnishings of the time when it was still called the Ungheria. Giuseppe Verdi and Richard Wagner with his wife Cosima and his father-in-law Franz Liszt were often to be seen here.

Other cafés and ice-cream parlours

Al Todaro, Piazzetta San Marco 3, San Marco
Chioggia, Piazzetta San Marco, San Marco 11
Foscarini, Accademia, Dorsoduro 878
Nico, Zattere ai Gesuiti, Dorsoduro 922
Paolin, Campo Santa Stefano, San Marco
Zorzi, Calle dei Fuseri, San Marco 4357

Camp Sites (campeggi)

Ca'Noghera

Camping Alba d'Oro
(a mile or so east of the airport)
tel. 5 41 51 02

Lido

Camping Adriatico
Via Sandro Gallo 215
tel. 96 67 70

Marghera

Camping Jolly Piscine
tel. 92 03 12

Camping Venezia
(4km east of Mestre)
tel. 97 59 28

Mestre

Camping Marco Polo
Via Triestina
tel. 5 41 53 46

Tessera

There are many other camp sites on the Cavallino peninsula (opposite the northern tip of the Lido).

Chemists (farmacie)

Summer: 8.30am–12.30pm, 4–8pm
Winter: 8.30am–12.30pm, 3.30–7.30pm

Opening times

Chemists that take it in turns to provide a service at night, on Sundays and public holidays are listed in the booklet "Un Ospite di Venezia" (A guest in Venice) and in the local paper "Il Gazzettino" under "Farmacia di turno". Helpline for the opening hours of chemists is 192.

Farmacia di turno

Consulate

P.O. Box 679 (Callers: Accademia 1051; tel. 5 22 72 07).

Great Britain

Currency

The unit of currency is the *lira* (plural *lire*).

Currency

There are banknotes for 1000, 2000, 5000, 10,000, 50,000, and 100,000 lire and coins in the denominations of 20, 50, 100, 200 and 500 lire.

The Italian parliament has been discussing currency reform for years. It is proposed to introduce a "new lira" which will be worth 1000 old lire. If and when the necessary legislation will be introduced remains uncertain. When the change takes place the old lira will remain in circulation with the new for two years.

Lira Nuova

There are no restrictions on the import of Italian and foreign currency into Italy, but in view of the strict controls on the export of currency it is advisable to declare any currency brought in on the appropriate form (*modulo V2*) at the frontier.

Import of currency

There is a limit of 20 million lire either in foreign currency or in Italian currency.

Export of currency

It is advisable to take money in the form of travellers' cheques, or to use Eurocheques with a Eurocheque card. Eurocheques can be used up to a value of 300,000 lire.

Travellers' cheques

Banks, the larger hotels and restaurants, car rental firms and many shops accept the leading international credit cards. The most widely used in Italy is Visa, followed by American Express, Eurocard and Diners Club.

Credit cards

See Banks

Changing money

Customs Regulations

Within the European Union the import and export of goods for private use is to a large extent free of customs duties. In order to distinguish between

EU

private and commercial use the following maximum amounts apply: 800 cigarettes, 400 cigarillos, 200 cigars, 1kg pipe tobacco, 10 litres of spirits, 20 litres of fortified wine, 90 litres of table wine (max. 60 litres of sparkling wine) and 110 litres of beer. In the event of spot checks, it is important to be able to show that the goods are essentially for private use.

The import of arms, imitation weapons, gas pistols, sheath knives, multi-purpose knives and tear-gas sprays is forbidden. Carrying any quantity of reserve fuel or filling fuel containers at petrol stations is also forbidden.

If it is necessary to import large amounts of money in the form of cash into Italy, the visitor is recommended to declare these sums on entry.

Bringing goods into Italy from outside the EU

Travellers to Italy from outside the EU aged 17 and over may bring in 200 duty-free cigarettes or 100 cigarillos or 50 cigars or 250g pipe tobacco, 2 litres each of table and sparkling wine, or 1 litre of spirits with more than 22% vol. of alcohol, 500g of coffee, or 200g of coffee extract, 100g of tea or 40g of tea extract, 50g of perfume or 0.25 litre of toilet water. Gifts not exceeding £175 in value are also duty-free.

Electricity

The voltage is 220V AC in most places, and Continental-type adaptors are required.

Events

The programme of events is published in the daily paper "Il Gazzettino" under local news and can also be obtained from tourist offices.

February

Carnevale: Venetian carnival

June

Biennale d'Arte: biennial art exhibition until September (1995, etc.)

July

Third Sunday in July: Festa del Redentore (Festival of the Redeemer) commemorating the end of the plague in 1576, culminating in an illuminated procession of gondolas and other craft on the Canale della Giudecca with music and fireworks (see A–Z, La Giudecca).

August

Film festival (until September)

September

First Sunday: Regatta storica, historical gondola regatta on the Canal Grande.

November

November 21st: Festa della Madonna della Salute, to commemorate the end of the plague in 1630. A large procession of pilgrims makes its way from the Basilica di San Marco (see A–Z) over a bridge of boats on the Canal Grande to the Church of Santa Maria della Salute (see A–Z).

Exursions

Lido

See A–Z, Lido

Punta Sabbioni/ Lido di Jésolo

From the Lido there is a motor-boat service (and also a car ferry) to Punta Sabbioni from which a road runs 20km/12½ miles north-east to the large resort of Lido di Jésolo which, with its beautiful broad beach, ranks with Rimini, Riccioni and the Venice Lido as one of the most popular resorts on the Adriatic.

See A–Z, Murano	Murano
See A–Z, Burano	Burano
See A–Z, Torcello	Torcello
See A–Z, Chioggia	Chioggia
Excursions to places around Venice can be booked in most travel agencies and hotels.	Where to book

First Aid (pronto soccorso)

Anywhere in Italy you can dial 113 for ambulance, fire or police.

Emergency service

Guardia Medica: at night and on public holidays tel. 93 73 66.

Emergency doctor on call

Pronto Soccorso Autoambulanze
Venice: tel. 52 30 00
Mestre: tel. 98 89 88

Blue Cross

Posto Pronto Soccorso
Venice: tel. 8 63 46
(San Marco 52)
Mestre: tel. 95 09 88

Red Cross
(Croce Rosso)

Ospedale al Mare;
tel. 5 26 17 50 (Lingomare d'Annunzio, 1, Lido)
Ospedale Gen. Prov. le Mestre;
tel. 98 89 88

Casualty departments
(Pronto Soccorso Accettazione Ammalati)

See entry

Chemists

See entry

Hospitals

Food and Drink

Although most hotels now serve a full continental breakfast, the Italians themselves are content with a quick espresso coffee in a bar and perhaps a cornetto (roll). Lunch and dinner are more substantial meals, typically consisting of a cold or hot starter (antipasto), with the next course (primo) usually pasta, followed by a main dish (secundo) of meat or fish, and ending with cheese (formaggio) and a dessert (dolce).

Meals

Lunch (pranzo or colazione) is usually between 1 and 3pm and dinner (cena) between 7 and 10pm.

Some Venetian specialities:

Brodetto di pesce: soup of fish from the Adriatic with onions, tomato juice, white wine, parsley, bay leaves and oil
Broèto: eel soup
Risi e luganega: rice soup with pork sausages

Soups (Minestre)

Cannelloni ripieni: tubular pieces of pasta filled with meat in a tomato sauce
Gnocchi alla Fontina: semolina dumplings with grated Fontina cheese
Gnocchi di patate: potato dumplings with a cheese sauce

Hors d'œuvres
(Antipasti)

Pappardelle con funghi: long noodles with mushrooms
Risi e bisi: rice with fresh peas and ham (the staple Venetian dish)
Risotto de peoci o de cape: rice with shellfish, crabs, shrimps, etc.
Soppressa: Venetian sausage
Spaghetti con vongole: spaghetti with clams

Meat dishes

Castradina alla griglia: grilled lamb
Fegato alla veneziana: calf's liver thinly sliced and cooked in butter with
    onions

Fish dishes

Anguille alla veneziana: eel cooked in a lemon and tuna sauce
Asia bolito: boiled whitefish
Baccala alla vicenta: salt cod simmered in milk
Coda di rospo al ferri: grilled anglerfish
Calamari fritti: squid rings fried in batter
Dorate: a fish from the Adriatic
Filetti di San Pietro fritti: fillets of St Peter's fish, coated in egg and flour and
    fried
Go: fish from the Venetian lagoon
Mansanete: fried crabs
Moleche: soft-shelled crayfish
Orate al ferri: grilled gilt-head bream
Seppie ai ferri con polenta: grilled small squid with maize flour cakes
Sogliola alla casserualo: casseroled sole with mushrooms
Triglie con risi: sea perch with rice

Drinks

Italians usually drink wine, especially local wines, with their meals, almost
always accompanied by mineral water.
    Strong black coffee (espresso) is drunk at the end of a meal, and is often
ordered "corrected" (corretto) with grappa or cognac.

Wine

Local white wines from Veneto include
Very dry (asciutto): Breganze bianco, Prosecco
Dry (secco): Bianco di Conliano, Gambellara
Fruity (abboccato): Barbarano bianco, Tokai, Verdiso
Medium dry: Soave
Sweet: Recioto

Sweet dessert wines: Moscato di Arqua, Prosecco Spumante

Local red wines from Veneto include
Very dry (asciutto): Barbarano rosso, Breganze rosse, Carbernet di Treviso,
    Friularo
Dry (secco): Bardolino, Merlot, Ricioto Amarone, Valpantena, Valpolicella
Fruity (abboccato), Redioto rosso, Rubino della Marca, Rubino del Piave

Restaurants

See entry

Galleries

Collezione Peggy Guggenheim
See A–Z, Ca'Venier dei Leoni

Galleria D'Arte Moderna
See A–Z, Palazzo Pesaro

Galleria d'Arte Moderna Graziussi
Campo San Fantin, San Marco 1998; tel. 5 28 50 81

Galleria d'Arte Moderna Il Traghetto
Campo S.M. del Giglio, San Marco 2460; tel. 5 22 11 88

Galleria d'Arte Naviglio Venezia
San Marco 1652; tel. 2 76 34

Galleria d'Arte Ravagnan
Piazza San Marco, San Marco 50/a; tel. 70 30 21

Galleria Franchetti
See A–Z, Ca'd'Oro

Galleria Luce Arte Moderna
San Marco 1922/a; tel. 5 22 29 49

Galleria Santo Stefano
Campo Santo Stefano, San Marco 2953; tel. 5 23 45 18

Galleria Totem – Il Canale
Accademia 878/b; tel. 5 22 36 41

Galleria dell'Accademia
See A–Z

Pinacoteca Manfrediniana
See A–Z, Seminario e Pinacoteca Manfrediniana

Pinacoteca di Palazzo Ducale
See A–Z, Palazzo Ducale (Doge's Palace)

Pinacoteca Querini-Stampalia
See A–Z, Palazzo Querini-Stampalia

Getting to Venice

Since 1933 the island city of Venice has been joined to the mainland by a road bridge (3.6km/2 miles), thus connecting Venice with the European motorway system via the autostrada from Milan to Trieste.

By car

The road bridge, the Ponte della Liberta, brings drivers into Venice where they can park on the island of Tronchetto (signposted: per Tronchetto) and near the Piazzale Roma in a multi-storey car park (Autorimessa Comunale) where there is also an accommodation bureau. There are also two other official car parks on the mainland to the north and south of the road bridge, namely, San Giuliano (motor boat 24 to the town) and Fusina (motor boat 16 to the town). If coming from Jésolo the best course is to leave the car at Punta Sabbioni and continue by boat or, if coming from the mainland, to park in Mestre or Marghera and then take the railway or the coach.

Parking

Tolls are payable on Italian motorways (autostrade). The charge is dependent on the cubic capacity and wheelbase of the vehicle. Auto-campers and cars towing a caravan have to pay almost double the normal rate for a car. A special credit card can be obtained which enables the driver to dispense with paying by cash at the toll-booth.

Motorways

Motorists should carry their driving licence and car registration document. An international insurance certificate ("green card") is not obligatory but is advisable. The car should have a nationality plate, and a warning triangle must be carried.

Documents, etc.

There is a wide choice of routes from the Channel Ports to Venice depending on individual preferences and time available – through France and over one of the Alpine passes into Italy; down the south coast of France and then

Roads to Venice

on the coastal motoway into Italy; by France or Germany, Switzerland and one of the Alpine passes or tunnels. The journey can be shortened by using one of the motorail services from stations in north-western Europe.

Frontier
crossings

Switzerland–Italy
The major frontier crossings open round the clock between Switzerland and Italy:

Great St Bernard Tunnel: Lausanne–Aosta–Turin
(The pass is generally closed from November to the end of March)

Simplon Tunnel: Brig–Iselle-Milan
Chiasso: Lugano–Como–Milan.
Castesegna/Chiavenna (Maloya Pass): St Moritz–Milan

Austria–Italy
The following frontier crossings between Austria and Italy are open round the clock:

Brenner Pass: Innsbruck–Bolzano
Reschen Pass: Landeck–Merano–Bolzano
Winnbach (Prato alle Drava): Lienz–Venice
Tarvisio: Villach–Udine–Venice

By coach

There are numerous package tours by coach either direct to Venice or including Venice on a longer circuit. For information apply to any travel agent.
Various coach companies also run services to Venice from Britain and northern Europe, including Eurolines which operates a regular service from London to Venice via Milan.

By air

There are scheduled flights from London to Venice daily and from Manchester to Venice weekly.
Marco Polo International Airport (Aeroporto Internazionale) is near Téssara. Buses run into Venice as far as the Air Terminal (Aerostazione), Fondamenta di Son Chiara near the Piazzale Roma (Canal Grande). There is a motor-boat service (motoscafi) to San Marco which takes 30 minutes.
Private flights land at Nicelli Airport (Aeroporto Nicelli) at San Nicolò di Lido (Lido) which has a motor-boat service to Riva degli Schiavoni (near San Marco).

Airlines

See Airport.

By sea

Venice is a favourite port of embarkation and has connections to all the major Adriatic ports plus Rhodes, Piraeus and Istanbul.
Cruise ships usually berth at Zattere or Riva degli Schiavoni. Information can be obtained from travel agencies or the Italian State Travel Office (see Tourist Information).

By rail

From London to Venice the fastest route, leaving London (Victoria) at 9am, takes just over 24 hours. Also, every Thursday (and sometimes Sunday) from mid March to mid November, the legendary Orient Express (restored) departs from London for Venice via Paris, Zurich and Innsbruck.

Arrival
in Venice

Since 1846 Venice has been connected to the mainland by a railway bridge linking its Santa Lucia Station to the international rail network. The station also has an accommodation booking service.

Hospitals (Ospedali)

Ospedale Civile:
Venice, Fondamenta dei Medicanti/Campo dei SS Giovanni e Paolo; tel. 0 78 45 16.

Ospedale Civile:
Mestre, Via Circonvallazione 50; tel. 95 79 44, 98 12 00

Ospedale al Mare:
Lido di Venezia, Ùngomare d'Annunzio 1; tel. 76 87 00

See First Aid

First Aid

See Insurance

Health
insurance

Hotels (Alberghi)

Hotels are officially classified in five categories, from luxury (5 stars) to hotels or pensions with modest amenities (1 star).

Categories

Room rates vary considerably according to season. The rates given in the following table (in lire) are based on information from the Italian State Tourist Office's list of hotels "Venezia 1995", but increases can be expected. Hotel bills should be kept in case of enquiry by Government Inspectors into possible tax evasion.

Rates

Receipted bills for accommodation and meals, etc. in Italian establishments must be retained and shown to a tax inspector on demand. Failure to do so entails a fine.

N.B.

Category	Single room Rate for 1 person	Double room Rate for 2 persons
★★★★★	180,000–480,000	220,000–700,000
★★★★	80,000–220,000	110,000–310,000
★★★	45,000–95,000	70,000–130,000
★★	25,000–45,000	40,000–75,000
★	20,000–35,000	30,000–60,000

Bauer Grünwald & Grand Hotel, Campo San Moisè, San Marco 1459; tel. 5 20 70 22; 219 r.
Cipriani, Giudecca 10; tel. 5 20 77 44; 98 r.
Danieli, Riva degli Schiavoni, Castello 4196; tel. 5 22 64 80; 245 r.
Europa & Regina, Via XXII Marzo, San Marco 2159; tel. 5 20 04 77; 199 r.
Gritti Palace, Campo Santa Maria del Giglio, San Marco 2467; tel. 79 46 11; 90 r.

City centre
★★★★★

Ala, Campo Santa Maria del Giglio, San Marco 2494; tel. 5 20 83 33; 78 r.
All'Angelo, Calle Larga San Marco, San Marco; tel. 5 20 92 99, 42 r.
Basilea, Rio Marin, Santa Croce 817; tel. 71 84 77; 38 r.
Bisanzio, Calle della Pietà, Castello 3651; tel. 5 20 31 00; 41 r.
Bonvecchiati, Calle Goldoni, San Marco 4488; tel. 5 28 50 17; 80 r.
Carlton Executive, S. Simeon Piccolo, Santa Croce 578; tel. 71 84 88; 125 r.
Carpaccio, Calle Corner, San Polo 2765; tel. 5 23 59 46; 13 r.
Cavaletto & Doge Orseolo, Calle Cavalleto, San Marco 1107; tel. 5 20 09 55; 82 r.
Gabrielli-Sandwirth, Riva degli Schiavoni, Castello 4110; tel. 5 23 15 80; 102 r.
Londra Palace, Riva degli Schiavoni, Castello 4171; tel. 5 20 05 33; 71 r.
Luna Baglioni, Calle Valleresso, San Marco, 1243; tel. 5 28 98 40; 123 r.
Metropole, Riva degli Schiavoni, Castello 4149; tel. 5 20 50 44; 64 r.
Monaco & Grand Canal, Calle Vallaresso, San Marco 1325; tel. 5 20 02 11; 77 r.
Principe, Lista di Spagna, Cannaregio 146; tel. 71 50 22, 154 r.
Pullman-Park Hotel, Fondamenta Condulmer, Santa Croce 245; tel. 5 28 53 94; 100 r.

★★★★

Hotel Bauer Grünwald

Saturnia & International, Via XXII Marzo, San Marco 2399; tel. 5 20 83 77; 109 r.

Star Hotel Splendid Suisse, Ponte dei Baretteri, San Marco 760; tel. 5 20 07 55; 166 r.

★★★ Ateneo, San Fantin, San Marco 1876; tel. 5 20 07 77; 20 r.
Continental & Corso, Lista di Spagna, Cannaregio 166; tel. 71 51 22; 104 r.
Flora, Via XXII Marzo, San Marco 2283/a; tel. 5 20 58 44; 43 r.
La Fenice et Des Artistes, Campiello de la Fenice, San Marco 1936; tel. 5 23 23 33; 62 r.
Montecarlo, Calle Specchieri, San Marco 463; tel. 5 20 71 44; 48 r.
Nazionale, Lista di Spagna, Cannaregio 158; tel. 71 61 33; 92 r.
Panada, Calle Specchieri, San Marco 646; tel. 5 20 90 88; 46 r.
San Marco, Piazza San Marco, San Marco 877; tel. 5 20 42 77; 57 r.
Savoia & Jolanda, Riva degli Schiavoni, Castello 4187; tel. 5 20 66 44; 62 r.

★★ Alla Salute-Da Cici, Fondamenta Ca'Balà, Dorsoduro 222; tel. 5 23 54 04; 37 r.
Dolomiti, Calle Priuli, Cannaregio 73; tel. 71 51 13; 24 r.
La Residenza, Campo Bandiera e Moro, Castello 3608; tel. 5 28 53 15; 14 r.
Paganelli, Riva degli Schiavoni, Castello 4182; tel. 5 22 43 24; 13 r.
Serenissima, Calle Goldoni, San Marco 4486; tel. 5 20 00 11; 31 r.

★ Belvedere, Via Garibaldi, Castello 1636; tel. 5 28 51 48; 12 r.
Marin, Calle del Traghetto, Santa Croce 670/b; tel. 71 80 22; 5 r.
Tintoretto, S. Fosca, Cannaregio 2316; tel. 72 15 22; 13 r.

Hotels on
the Lido
★★★★★ Excelsior, Lungomare Marconi 41; tel. 5 26 02 01; 222 r.

★★★★ Des Bains, Lungomare Marconi 17; tel. 5 26 59 21; 195 r.
Le Boulevard, Gran Viale S.M. Elisabetta; tel. 5 26 19 90; 49 r.

Hotel Europa & Regina

Hotel Gritti Palace

Quattro Fontane, Via 4 Fontane 16; tel. 5 26 02 27; 69 r.
Villa Laguna, Via San Gallo 6; tel. 5 26 03 42; 31 r.
Villa Mabapa, Riviera S. Nicolò 16; tel. 5 26 05 90; 61 r.

Atlanta-Augustus, Via Lepanto 15; tel. 5 26 05 69; 31 r. ★★★
Belvedere, Via Cerigo 1; tel. 5 26 01 15; 29 r.
Biasutti Adria Urania-Nora & Villa Ada (17 r.), Via E. Dandolo 29;
  tel. 5 26 01 20; 20 r.
Helvetia, Gran Viale 4/6; tel. 5 26 01 05; 50 r.
Petit Palais, Lungomare Marconi 54; tel. 5 26 59 93, 27 r.
Rigel, Via E. Dandolo 13; tel. 5 26 88 10; 42 r.
Villa Otello, Via Lepanto 12; tel. 5 26 00 48; 34 r.
Villa Parco, Via Rodi 1; tel. 5 26 00 15; 23 r.

Rieter, Gran Viale 57/b; tel. 5 26 01 07; 29 r. ★★
Sorriso, Via Colombo 22/c; tel. 5 26 07 29; 49 r.
Villa Pannonia, Via D. Michiel 48; tel. 5 26 01 62; 30 r.
Villa Tiziana, Via Andrea Gritti 3; tel. 5 26 11 52; 18 r.

La Pergola, Via Cipro 15; tel. 5 26 07 84; 17 r. ★
Villa della Palme, Via E. Dandolo 12; tel. 5 26 13 12; 11 r.

Albatros, Viale Don Sturzo 32; tel. 61 10 00; 152 r. Hotels in Mestre
Ambasciatori, Corso del Popolo 221; tel. 5 31 06 99; 97 r. ★★★★★
Bologna & Statione, Via Piave 214; tel. 93 10 00; 134 r.
Michelangelo, Via Forte Marghera 69; tel. 98 66 00; 54 r.
Plaza, Piazzale Stazione 36; tel. 92 93 88; 230 r.
Ramada, Via Orlanda 4; tel. 5 31 05 00; 181 r.

Aurora, Piazza G. Bruno 16; tel. 98 91 88; 29 r. ★★★
Capitol, Via Orlanda 1; tel. 5 31 24 47; 89 r.
President, Via Forte Marghera 99/a; tel. 98 56 55; 55 r.

San Giuliano, Via Forte Marghera 193/a; tel. 5 31 70 44; 46 r.
Venezia, Via Teatro Vecchio 5; tel. 98 55 33; 100 r.

★★ Ariston, Via Terraglio 11/c; tel. 97 22 93; 45 r.
Centrale, Piazzale Donatori di Sangue 15; tel. 98 55 22; 69 r.
Trieste, Piazzale Stazione 2; tel. 92 12 44
Vivit, Piazza Ferretto 75; tel. 95 13 85; 19 r.

★ Adria, Via Cappuccina 34; tel. 98 97 55; 20 r.
Alla Torre, Cale del Sale 54; tel. 98 46 46; 2 r.
Col di Lana, Via Fagarè 19; tel. 90 00 64; 4 r.

Insurance

Car insurance — Although not a legal requirement for citizens of EU countries it is extremely advisable to have an international insurance certificate (green card). It is also important to have fully comprehensive cover and, since Italian insurance companies tend to be slow in settling claims, it is wise to take out short-term insurance against legal costs if these are not already covered.

Health insurance — British visitors to Italy, in common with other EU citizens, are entitled to receive health care on the same basis as Italians (including free medical treatment, etc.), and should get a certificate of entitlement (Form E111) from their local social security office well before their date of departure. Fuller cover can be obtained by taking out insurance against medical expenses. Non-EU citizens will, of course, be well advised to take out appropriate insurance cover.

Baggage insurance — In view of the risk of theft it is wise to have adequate insurance against baggage loss or damage.

Language

Italian — As the direct descendant of Latin, Italian comes closer to it than any of the other Romance languages. Italian had many dialects, not least because of the country's past political divisions, but the great 13th/14th c. writers, especially Dante, used Tuscan and this is still the recognised medium of communication.

Venetian dialect — The Venetians speak a distinctive Italian dialect of their own. Not only is their pronunciation more softened than in any other part of the country, they also change actual words of Italian: brothers, for example is "frari" instead of "frati", house is "ca" instead of "casa", angel "anzelo" instead of "angelo" and fish is "pesse" instead of "pesce".

The Venetian dialect is also found throughout Venice on the nameplates of streets, canals, buildings, etc.

Pronunciation — The stress is usually on the penultimate syllable. Where it falls on the last syllable this is always indicated by an accent (perché, città). Where the stress is on the last syllable but two an accent is not officially required, except in certain doubtful cases, but it is sometimes shown as an aid to pronunciation.

Consonants: c before c or i is pronounced ch, otherwise like k; g before e or i is pronounced like j, otherwise hard (as in "go"); gn and gl are like n and l followed by a consonantal y (roughly as in "onion" and "million"); h is silent, qu as in English, r is rolled; s is unvoiced (as in "so") at the beginning of a word before a vowel, but has the sound of z between vowels and before b, d, g, l, m, n and vv; sc before e or i is pronounced sh; z is either like ts or ds. Vowels are pronounced in the "continental" fashion, without the diphthongisation normal in English; e is never silent. The vowels in a diphthong are pronounced separately (ca-usa, se-i).

Good morning, good day!	Buon giorno!	Everyday expressions
Good evening!	Buona sera!	
Goodbye	Arrivederci	
Yes, no	Si, no!	
I beg your pardon	Scusí	
Please	Per favore	
Thank you (very much)	(Molte)gracie!	
Not at all (you're welcome)	Prego	
Excuse me (when passing in front of someone)	Con permesso	
Do you speak English?	Parla inglese?	
A little, not much	Un poco, non molto	
I do not understand	Non capisco	
What is the Italian for . . .?	Come si dice . . . in italiano?	
What is the name of this church?	Come si chiama questa chiesa?	
The cathedral	Il duomo	
The square	La piazza	
The palace	Il palazzo	
The theatre	Il teatro	
Where is the Via . . .?	Dov'è la via . . .?	
Where is the road (motorway) to . . .?	Dov'è la strada (autostrada) per . . .?	
Left, right	A sinistra, a destra	
Straight ahead	Sempre diritto	
Above, below	Sopra, sotto	
When is (it) open?	Quando è aperto?	
How far is it?	Quanto è distante?	
Today	Oggi	
Yesterday	Ieri	
The day before yesterday	L'altro ieri	
Tomorrow	Domani	
Have you any rooms?	Ci sono camere libre?	
I should like . . .	Vorrei avere . . .	
A room with bath (shower)	Una camera con bagno (doccia)	
With full board	Con pensione completa	
What does it cost	Qual'è il prezzo? Quanto costa?	
All-in (price)	Tutto compreso	
That is too dear	E troppo caro	
Bill, please (to a waiter)	Cameriere, il conto!	
Where are the lavatories	Dove si trovano i gabinetti? (il servizi, la ritrata)	
Wake me at six	Può svegliarmi alle sei!	
Where is there a doctor (dentist)?	Dove sta un medico (un dentista)?	
Address	Indirizzo	At the post office
Airmail	Posta aerea	
Express	Espresso	
Letter	Lettera	
Post box	Buca delle lettere	
Postcard	Cartolina	
Poste restante	Fermo posta	
Postman	Postino	
Stamp	Francobollo	
Registered letter	Lettera raccomandata	
Telegram	Telegramma	
Telephone	Telefono	

Libraries

Travelling		
	Aircraft	Aeroplano
	Airport	Aeroporto
	Arrival	Arrivo
	Baggage (luggage)	Bagagli
	Booking office	Sportello
	Bus (tram) stop	Fermata
	Change (trains)	Cambiare treno
	Departure (air)	Partenza (Decollo)
	Departure (rail)	Partenza
	Fare	Prezzo di biglietto (Tariffa)
	Flight	Volo
	No smoking	Vietato fumare
	Guard	Capotreno
	Platform	Marciapiede
	Porter	Portabagagli (faccino)
	Station	Stazione
	Stop	Sosta
	Ticket collector	Conduttore
	Timetable	Orario
	Track	Binario
	Waiting room	Sala d'aspetto
Days of the week		
	Monday	Lunedi
	Tuesday	Martedi
	Wednesday	Mercoledi
	Thursday	Giovedi
	Friday	Venerdi
	Saturday	Sabato
	Sunday	Domenica
	Day	Giorno
	Weekday	Giorno feriale
	Holiday	Giorno festivo
	Week	Settimana
Holidays		
	New year	Capo d'anno
	Easter	Pasqua
	Whitsun	Pentecoste
	Christmas	Natale
Months		
	January	Gennaio
	February	Febbraio
	March	Marzo
	April	Aprile
	May	Maggio
	June	Giugno
	July	Luglio
	August	Agosto
	September	Settembre
	October	Ottobre
	November	Novembre
	December	Dicembre

Libraries

Biblioteca Nazionale Marciana
See A–Z, Libreria Vecchia di San Marco
(exhibition rooms)

Biblioteca Querini-Stampalia
See A–Z, Palazzo Querini-Stampalia

Collezione della Fondazione Giorgio Cini
See A–Z, San Giorgio Maggiore
The collection of the Monastery of San Giorgio Maggiore can only be seen
by prior appointment.

Raccolte dei Padri Armeni Mechitaristi
San Lazzaro degli Armeni (island)
Open Mon.–Sat. 3.30–5pm
Collection of pictures, books and manuscripts.

Lost Property Offices (servizi oggetti rinvenuti)

Riva del Carbon, Pallazzo Farsetti (city hall), Campo San Luca;
tel. 5 20 88 44

Municipal lost
property office

ACNIL (city public transport) lost property office; tel. 78 03 10

Municipal
transport

Santa Lucia Station; tel. 71 61 22, ex 3238

Rail station

Aeroporto Marco Polo; tel. 66 12 66

Airport

Markets (mercati)

Pescheria. See A–Z, Pescheria

Erberia
Canal Grande (near the fish market)
Boats unload fruit and vegetables here in the late afternoon.

Fruit market
Campo Santa Maria Formosa

Motoring

In general traffic regulations in Italy do not differ essentially from those in
other European countries where vehicles travel on the right. Traffic signs
are those internationally agreed.

Within built-up areas: 50kph/30mph.
    On main roads outside built-up areas: cars and motor cycles 90–
110kph/56–65mph; cars with trailers, caravans and campers 80kph/50mph.
    Motorways: cars and motor cycles 130kph/80mph; cars with trailers,
caravans and campers 100kph/62mph.
    In fog or conditions of visibility under 100m/110yd vehicle speeds must
not exceed 50kph/30mph.
    In the event of a speeding infringement there is the likelihood of a
substantial fine and even the loss of the driver's licence.

Speed limits

All car occupants over 14 years of age must wear a seat belt. Children under
four years of age must travel in special children's seats.

Seat belts,
Children in
cars

All motorists must carry a warning triangle and it is recommended that
visitors equip themselves with a spare set of light bulbs.

Compulsory
equipment

Traffic on main roads has priority where the road is marked with the priority
sign (a square with the corner pointing downwards, coloured white with a

Priority

red border or yellow with a black and white border). Otherwise (even on roundabouts) the rule is "right before left". On narrow mountain roads traffic going up has priority. Trams always have priority.

Overtaking	A change of lane both before and after overtaking or for any other purpose must be signalled with the direction indicators; in addition, outside built-up areas the horn must also be sounded during daylight. After dark headlamps must be flashed for the same purpose.
Prohibition on use of horn	In towns the use of the horn is frequently prohibited, either by an appropriate road sign (a horn with a stroke through it) or by a sign saying "Zona di silenzio".
Lights	On well-lit roads just sidelights may be used apart from in tunnels and galleries where dipped headlights must be used at all times.
Zebra crossings	Pedestrians have absolute priority on zebra crossings.
Traffic police	The directions of the traffic police (*polizia stradale*) should be complied with implicitly; traffic offences are subject to heavy fines.
Drunk driving	There are heavy penalties for driving under the influence of drink.
Spare cans	Carrying spare cans of petrol in a vehicle is prohibited.
Unleaded fuel	Unleaded motor fuel is available from most filling stations in Northern Italy.
Accidents	In the event of an accident make sure you have all the necessary particulars and supporting evidence (statements by witnesses, sketches, photographs, etc.) If the accident involves personal injury it must be reported to the police. You should notify your own personal insurance company as soon as possible, and if you are responsible or partly responsible for the accident you should also inform the Italian insurance company or bureau whose address is given on your "green card". They will give advice and supply the name of a lawyer should you be subject to legal proceedings. If your car is a total write-off the Italian Customs authorities must be informed at once, since otherwise you might be required to pay the full import duty on the vehicle.
Automobile clubs	Automobile Club d'Italia (ACI) Venice branch office: Fondamenta Son Chiara, Piazzale Roma 518a; tel. 70 03 00 Mestre branch office: Via Ca' Marcello 67a; tel. 5 31 03 62
Breakdown service	In the event of a breakdown on the road anywhere in Italy just call 116 from the nearest public telephone. Tell the operator where you are, give your vehicle make and registration number, and the nearest ACI office will be notified for immediate assistance.
Puncture repair	Look for the sign "Riparazione Gomme".
Repair garages	Look for "Officina".
Police and ambulance	Tel. 113 anywhere in Italy

Museums

Casa Goldoni (Palazzo Centani)
Campo San Tomà, San Polo 2794
Open: Mon.–Sat. 8.30am–1.30pm

The birthplace of 18th c. Venetian playwright Carlo Goldoni (see Famous People), the house contains personal memorabilia as well as interesting exhibits on theatre history. This is also the site of a theatre institute.

Collezione Cini (Palazzo Cini)
San Vio, Dorsoduro 864
Open: daily except Mon. 2–7pm; closed in winter.
Collection of Tuscan art of the 13th–16th c.; pictures, furniture, ivory carvings.

Museo Archeologico
See A–Z

Museo d'Arte Orientale
See A–Z, Palazzo Pesaro

Museo d'Arte Vetraria (glass museum)
See A–Z, Murano

Museo Civico Correr
See A–Z

Museo della Comunità Israelitica (Jewish museum)
See A–Z, Il Ghetto

Museo Diocesano (Diocesan museum)
Fondamenta S. Apollonia (in the former Sant'Apollonia monastery), Castello 4312
Open: daily 10.30am–12.30pm
Among the treasures of the museum are liturgical articles, silverwork and paintings. The exhibits in the department of contemporary sacred art range from architectural sketches to stained glass.

Museo dell'Estuario Torcello
Open: daily except Mon. 10am–12.30pm and 2–5.30pm
Exhibits concerning history of Torcello from antiquity to 16th c.

Museo Fortuny
Campo San Beneto, San Marco 3780
Open: daily except Mon. 9am–7pm
Collection of textiles, paintings, theatrical costumes and furniture, including work by set designer Mariano Fortuny

Museo di Icone dell'Istituto Ellenico (icon museum)
See A–Z

Museo Marciano (Museum of San Marco)
See A–Z, Basilica di San Marco

Museo dell'Opera di Palazzo Ducale
See A–Z, Palazzo Ducale

Museo del Risorgimento (museum of Italian unification movement)
See A–Z, Museo Civico Correr

Museo dei Settecento Veneziano (museum of Venice in the 18th c.)
See A–Z, Palazzo Rezzonico

Museo di Storia Naturale (natural history museum)
See A–Z, Fondaco dei Turchi

Museo Storico Navale (maritime museum)
See A–Z

Museums

Pinacoteca Manfrediniana
See A–Z, Seminario Pinacoteca Manfrediniana

Pinacoteca Querini-Stampalia
See A–Z, Palazzo Querini-Stampalia

Galleries
See entry

Opening times
Since Italian museum opening times are frequently altered, the times given here cannot be guaranteed. To avoid disappointment it is best to check on them beforehand when planning to visit a particular museum.

Music

Opera/ballet
Teatro La Fenice, Campo San Fantin
See A–Z, Teatro La Fenice

Concerts
Conservatorio di Musica Benedetto Marcello,
Santo Stefano 2810

Musical performances
Palazzo Labia
Fondamenta Labia
Motor boat: 1 (to San Marcuola)
RAI, the Italian radio station, occasionally puts on concerts.

Gondola serenades
Musical gondola trips on the Canal Grande from May to September, departing at 9pm from Bauer-Grünwald Hotel.
Advance booking: CIT, Piazza San Marco

Nightlife

Casino
Casino Municipale:
From October to March in the Palazzo Vendramin-Calergi,
Canal Grande, Cannaregio 2040; tel. 71 02 11
From April to September in the Palazzo del Casino, Lungomare G.
Marconi 4, Lido; tel. 76 06 26

Motor launches: there are two motor launches (motoscafo diretto) as well as the motor-boat service between the Casino on the Lido and the main railway station, the Piazzale Roma (Fondamenta San Chiara) and San Marco (Giardini).

Night time entertainment
Among the best known places are:
Antico Pignolo, Calle Specchieri, San Marco 451
Ai Musicanti, Ponte della Canonica, Castello 4309
Blue Moon, Lido, Piazzale Sergher
Casanova, Calle larga Vendramin, Cannaregio
Martini Scala, Calle de Cafetier, San Marco 2007
Night Club Antico Martini, San Marco 1880
Parco delle Rose, Lido, Gran Viale
La Perla, Lido, Lungomare Marconi 4

Opening times

Shops
Generally: Mon.–Sat. 9am–1pm and 3.30–7.30pm; July–September:
Mon.–Sat. 9am–1pm and 4–8pm

Closed:
foodshops: Monday morning
other shops: Wednesday afternoon
hairdressers: Monday

The opening times are given under the entry for each museum (see A–Z and Practical Information, Museums). Most museums are closed on public holidays as well as the day when they are normally closed. Since opening times are frequently subject to alteration and there are often additional closures due to staff shortages, strikes, renovation, etc., it is advisable to check in advance whether a museum will be open.

Museums

The large churches are usually open until noon and for the most part also from 4 or 5pm until dusk; some of the major churches are open all day. It is possible to see the interior of a church during a service if care is taken to avoid disturbing the worshippers. Visitors should always be suitably dressed, avoiding sleeveless dresses or blouses, miniskirts, shorts, short-sleeved shirts, etc. If inappropriately dressed they may be refused admittance; cover-up garments can be hired at the entrance of some churches.
   During Lent almost all altarpieces are covered and not shown to visitors.

Churches

See entry

Banks

See Postal Services

Post Offices

Palaces (palazzi)

Venice has over 900 palaces. Although totally different in style, furnishings and size, they have one thing in common: every palace has one main façade, overlooking either a canal or a campo; the other three sides are uninteresting, plain and often almost shabby. This applies particularly to the palaces on the Canal Grande which means there is no point in looking for the street entrance to a palace unless it houses a museum or a gallery.
   For all the other palaces (and that is about 80% of them) it is enough just to look at their principal façade from a boat on one of the canals.
   A good way to gain at least a first impression of the imposing façades on both sides of the Canal Grande is to take Line 1, the boat service that plies the whole length of the Canal Grande, with stopping-off points at frequent intervals (see Sightseeing tours).

Police (carabiniere)

Police Headquarters, Passport and Aliens Department; tel. 5 20 32 22

Questura

Venice: tel. 113
Mestre: tel. 5 77 77

Accident

Traffic police, Mestre, Via Ca' Rossa 14; tel. 96 17 22, 5 61 11

Polizia Stradale

Municipal police:
Palazzo Loredan; tel. 5 22 40 63
Piazzale Roma; tel. 5 22 26 12, 5 22 45 76
Lido: Via Sandro Gallo; tel. 5 26 03 95
Mestre: Via Slongo 22; tel. 5 05 61 03

Vigili Urbani

Emergency service (pronto intervento):
Venice and Mestre; tel. 112

Carabinieri

Postal Services

Letters within Italy and to EU countries 850 lire; postcards 750 lire

Postal rates

Italian postbox

Telephone

Stamps (francobolli)	Stamps can be bought at post offices, at tobacconists' (indicated by a large T above the door) and from stamp machines.
Head Post Office	Palazzo Fondaco dei Teschi (near the Ponte di Rialto) This is the only post office that can be used for poste restante. Open: Mon.–Sat. 9am–8pm; Sun. 9am–noon. Other post offices are open Mon.–Fri. 8.15am–1.30pm, Sat. 8.30am–noon.
Telegrams (day and night)	Ufficio Principale Telegrafico Centrale (Head Post Office) Stazione Santa Lucia (main railway station) Poste e Telegrafi, Calle dell'Ascensione Open: Mon.–Fri. 8.15am–1.45pm Telegrams by telephone: tel. 186

Public Holidays

1 January (New Year's Day); 6 January (Epiphany); Easter; 25 April (Liberation Day, 1945); 1 May (Labour Day); 1st Sunday in June (Proclamation of the Republic); 15 August (Assumption: a family celebration, the high point of the Italian summer holiday migration); 1 November (All Saints); 1st Sunday in November (Day of National Unity); 8 December (Immaculate Conception); 25 and 26 December (Christmas).

Public Transport

Lagoon Services — Vaporetti (canal steamers), motoscafi (motor launches) and motonavi (motor boats) provide Venice with its public transport, operating between the different parts of the city and also connecting the city with the islands.

Historic gondola regatta on the Canal Grande ▶

Public Transport

Operating times of the individual vaporetto services differ; most of them, however, run at least from 6am to 11pm; a few (e.g. Line 1) operate throughout the night, but only hourly after 1am.

Fares

The fares depend on the length of the journey and on the time of day.

Information

A free map giving information on all public transport can be obtained from the information offices (see Tourist Information).

Permanent transport routes

Linea 1
Piazzale Roma–Ferrovia–Canal Grande–Lido (and vice versa)
Stops:
1 Piazzale Roma–2 Ferrovia–3 Riva di Biasio–4 S. Marcuola–5 S. Staè–6 Ca' D'Oro–7 Rialto–8 S. Silvestro–9 S. Angelo–10 S. Tomà–11 Ca' Rezzonico–12 Accademia–13 S. Maria del Giglio–14 Salute–16 S. Marco–17 Arsenale–18 Giardini–19 S. Elena–20 Lido

Linea 6
Riva degli Schiavoni–Lido (and vice versa)
Direct Line (Linea diretta)

Linea 10
Riva degli Schiavoni–Ospedali lagunari (and vice versa)

Linea 12
Fondamente Nuove–Murano–Mazzorbo–Burano (and vice versa)

Linea 13
Fondamente Nuove–Murano–Vignole–S. Erasmo (and vice versa)

Linea 14
Riva degli Schiavoni–Lido–Punta Sabbioni–Treporti–Burano–Torcello (and vice versa)

Linea 17
Ferry Boat: Venezia (Tronchetto)–Lido (S. Nicolò) (and vice versa)

Linea 20
Riva degli Schiavoni–S. Lazzaro (and vice versa)

Linea 52
Zitelle–S. Zaccaria–Murano–Lido
Stops:
S. Zaccaria–Fondamente Nuove–S. Michele (Cimitero)–Murano–Fondamente Nuove–Madonna dell'Orto–S. Alvise–Pontre Tre Archi–Ferrovia–Piazzale Roma–Zattere–Giudecca–S. Zaccaria–Lido (and vice versa)

Linea 82
S. Marco–Canal Grande–Tronchetto–Giudecca–S. Zaccaria (and vice versa)

Seasonal tourist lines

Linea 3
S. Zaccaria–Canale della Giudecca–Tronchetto–Ferrovia–Rialto–S. Samuele–S. Marco–S. Zaccaria (circular line mornings only)

Linea 4
S. Zaccaria–S. Marco–S. Samuele–Rialto–Ferrovia–Tronchetto–Canale della Giudecca–S. Zaccaria (circular line afternoons only)

Linea 16
Fusina–Zattere (and vice versa)

Linea 17
Lido (S. Niccolò)–Punta Sabbioni (and vice versa)

Linea 52
Lido (S.M. Elisabetta)–Casino (and vice versa)

Linea 82
S. Zaccaria–Lido (and vice versa)

Linea 5
Venezia (Piazzale Roma)–Aeroporto Marco Polo (and vice versa)

Linee 2, 4, 7, 12, 19
Venezia (Piazzale Roma)–Mestre (and vice versa)

Linea 6
Venezia (Piazzale Roma)–Marghera (and vice versa)

Main landing-stages: by the railway station and on the Molo, in front of the Piazzetta
   Gondolas are usually hired by the hour. There is an extra charge for luggage.

Gondolas

The motor launches can be hired for a tour of the city or for trips round the lagoon. There is also an extra charge for luggage.
   They also operate a regular service from the railway station or the Piazzale Roma to the Ponte di Rialto and to the hotels round San Marco and on the Lido.

Boat hire (motoscafi di nolo)

Buses provide transport between Venice and the mainland. On the Lido, buses operate between the landing-stages at San Niccolò and Santa Maria Elisabetta and Lungomare Marconi (Route A) and between Santa Maria Elisabetta and the public beaches and Citta Giordana (Route B) or alternatively Alberoni (Route C).
   There is also a route connecting Santa Maria Elisabetta with Alberoni, San Pietro in Volta and Pellestrina (Route 11).

Buses

Radio

Information on BBC overseas radio transmissions in English is available from BBC External Services, P.O. Box 76, Bush House, London WC2B 4PH; tel. 0171 240 3456.

Programmes in English

The Italian Radio Service (RAI) broadcasts a number of programmes for foreign tourists (news, commentaries, etc.) in the holiday season in various languages including English.

The first national programme of the radio service (RAI; medium wave and VHF) puts out travel information daily at 1.56pm (also in English).

Travel information

Rail Services

The Italian railway system covers a total of 16,000km/10,000 miles, most of it run by the Italian State Railways (Ferrovie dello Stato; FS).

Ferrovie dello Stato (FS)

Information about rail services is obtainable from the Italian State Tourist Office or from Italian State Railways offices abroad:

CIT, Marco Polo House, 3/5 Lansdown Road, Croydon, Surrey; tel. 0181 686 0677

United Kingdom

127

Rail Services

United States of America	765 Route 83, Suite 105, Chicago Ill
	5670 Wilshire Boulevard, Los Angeles, Cal.
	668 Fifth Avenue, New York, NY

Canada
2055 Peel Street, Suite 102, Montreal
111 Richmond Street West, Suite 419, Toronto

Italian State Railways has offices in towns throughout Italy.

Venice
48 Piazza San Marco (in the parade near the Campanile)
Open: Mon.–Fri. 8.30am–12.30pm, 3–6.30pm; Sat. 8.30am–12.30pm
Closed Sun., public holidays

Tickets
The validity of tickets on Italian Railways depends on the length of the journey, from 1 day (up to 250km/155 miles) to 6 days (over 1000km/620 miles).

Tourist ticket
The tourist ticket (TAW: Travel at Will) allows the holder to make an unlimited number of journeys in first or second class on the entire Italian rail network within periods of 8, 15, 21 or 30 days.

Kilometric ticket
With this ticket up to five persons can make up to 20 different single journeys totalling not more than 3000km.

Children's tickets
Children under 4, accompanied by an adult and not occupying a seat, travel free. Children under 12 occupying a seat pay half fare.

Inter-Rail ticket
Young people under 26 who purchase an Inter-Rail ticket can travel in Italy without any other ticket and at considerably reduced fares. This ticket is valid for a month in second class.
   Young people under 26 holding Twen-tickets are also entitled to a reduction.

Reductions for senior citizens
Senior citizens (over 60 years of age) who hold both a Senior Citizen's card issued in their home country and a RES (Rail Europ Senior) card are entitled to a 30% reduction in fares. Both cards have the same period of validity.

Restaurants

Selection
★Antico Martini, Campo San Fantin, San Marco 1983; tel. 5 23 70 27
★Do Forni, Calle dei Specchieri, San Marco 457/468; tel. 5 23 77 29
★Gritti, Campo Santa Maria del Giglio, San Marco 2467; tel. 5 22 60 44
★Osteria da Fiore, Calle del Scaleter, San Polo 2202; tel. 72 13 08
★Taverna La Fenice, Campiello della Fenice, San Marco 1938; tel. 5 23 78 66
Al Colombo, Campiello del Teatro Goldoni, San Marco 4619; tel. 5 23 74 98
Al Conte Pescator, Piscina San Zulian, San Marco 544; tel. 5 22 14 83
Al Giardinetto, Ruga Giuffa, Castello 4928; tel. 5 28 53 32
Al Giglio, Campo S.M. del Giglio, San Marco 2477; tel. 8 94 56
Al Graspo de UA, Calle dei Bombaseri, San Marco 5093; tel. 5 22 36 47
Antica Carbonera, Calle Bembo, San Marco 4648; tel. 2 54 79
Da Bruno, Calle del Paradiso, Castello 5731; tel. 5 22 14 80
Fiaschetteria Toscana, San Giovanni Crisostomo, Cannaregio 5719;
   tel. 5 28 52 81
Harry's Bar, Calle Vallaresso, San Marco 1323; tel. 5 23 67 97
Harry's Dolci, Giudecca 773; tel. 5 22 48 44
La Caravella, Calle XXII Marzo, San Marco 2397; tel. 5 20 89 01
La Colomba, Piscina Frezzeria, San Marco 1665; tel. 5 22 11 75
La Regina, Calle della Regina, Santa Croce 2330; tel. 5 24 14 02
Montin, Fondamenta della Eremite, Dorsoduro 1147; tel. 2 71 51
Noemi, Calle dei Fabbri, San Marco 912; tel. 2 52 38

Every restaurant must give customers a receipted bill; this must be shown
on demand to a tax inspector in the vicinity of the restaurant. Failure to do
so can be subject to a fine.

Meals "à la carte" are expensive, so the "menu turistico", which is usually
very good, is well worth recommending. Besides the often relatively
expensive and lavish "ristorante" Italy has many usually modest but good
quality establishments known as "osteria" (originally country inns serving
wine and plain fare) and "trattoria" (an urban variant of an osteria, generally serving typical regional food). If you want to eat in a hurry look for a
"pizzeria" or a "tavola calda" or "rosticceria" (both rather like a cafeteria).
As a general rule, the further you are from St Mark's Square, the lower the
prices.

Customers must always be on their guard against being overcharged or
being served with something they have not ordered. This is especially true
of fish restaurants. If you are surprised at a figure on the bill which is not the
same as on the menu you may be told that you have been served with a
particularly large lobster, etc. If this is not what you ordered have no
compunction about refusing and sending for the police if necessary.

Shopping

Venice is excellent for buying leather goods, textiles, glassware, gold and
silver items, and of course Venetian lace (especially lace embroidery from
Burano). A stroll around the Merceria (see A–Z), the Frezzeria (behind the
Piazza San Marco, second street running parallel to the Napoleon wing),
the Rialto Bridge or the arcades off St Mark's Square will give you a good
idea of what is on offer. Here there are plenty of special souvenirs on sale
but it is worth noting that the prices can be comparatively high.

Shopping streets

Antiquario Casellati
Calle XXII Marzo, San Marco 2404

Antiques

Frezzati
Calle Larga XXII Marzo, San Marco 2070

Scarpa,
Calle Larga XXII Marzo, San Marco 2089

Bertoni,
Calle della Mandola, San Marco 3637b

Fantoni,
Salizzada San Luca, San Marco 4119

Filippi
Calle della Bissa, San Marco 5458
Calle del Paradiso, Castello 5763

Al Canale
Ruga Rialto, San Polo 973

Arts and Crafts

Goldoni
Calle dei Fabbri, San Marco 4742/43

Books

Sansovino
Bacino Orseolo, San Marco 84

Serenissima,
Mercerie San Zulian, San Marco 739

Shopping

Hand-crafted masks at Mondonovo . . .   *. . . and in the La Mano workshop*

Fashions

Elysée Due
Frezzeria, San Marco 1693

Fiorella Show, Campo San Stefano,
San Marco 2806

Gian Franco Ferre
Calle Larga San Marco, San Marco 287

Krizia
Via XXII Marzo, San Marco 2359

La Coupole
Frezzeria, San Marco 1674
Calle Larga XXII Marzo, San Marco 2366

Laura Biagiotti
(near the Theatre Goldoni), San Marco 4600/a

Missoni
Calle Vallaresso, San Marco 1312

Roberta di Camerino
Ascensione, San Marco 1255/1256

Valentino
Salizada San Moisèe, San Marco 1473

Glass

CAM
Piazzale Colonna 1/B
Murano

... *elaborate glasswork of Salviati*

... *or the crazy fashion of Fiorella*

Ferro & LLazzarini
Fondamenta Navagero 75
Murano

Gino Cedendese
Piazza San Marco 139
Fondamenta Venier 48, Murano

Salviati
Piazza San Marco, San Marco 78

La Buata
Mercerie, San Marco 260

Jewellery

Pandora Jewellery
Calle dei Fuseri, San Marco 4469

See A–Z, Burano

Lace

Jesurum
Ponte Canonica, San Marco

Kerer
Calle Canonica, Castello 4328a

Maria Mazzaron
Fondamenta dell'Osmarin, Castello 4970

Bussola
(near Theatre Goldoni) San Marco 4608

Leather

La Bauta
Mercurie San Zulian, San Marco 729

	Vogini (near Piazza San Marco), San Marco 1257
Marbled paper (papier à cuve)	Legatoria Piazzesi Campiello della Feltrina, San Marco 2511
	Il Papiro San Marco 2764
Masks	La Mano (5 studios) Calle Longa S.M. Formosa, Castello 5175 Rio Terrà dei Biri, Cannaregio 5415 Barbaria de la Tole, Castello 6468/6469 Ruga Rialto, S. Polo 1032 Calle Fiubera, San Marco 818
Shoes	Casella, San Marco 5048
	Franz, San Marco 4578a
	La Fenice Via XXII Marzo, San Marco 2255
Sports goods	Corner Shop, San Marco 4855
	Zeta Sport Calle dei Fabbri, San Marco 4668
Markets	See entry
Opening times	See entry

Sightseeing

City tours	Check with the travel agencies (see entry) who organise guided tours or with tourist offices (see Tourist Information).
Canal tours	A sightseeing tour Venetian-style is a boat ride along the Grand Canal from the railway station to the Piazza di San Marco. You can choose between taking it easy on the "slow boat" (Accelerato No. 1), calling at every stop, and the Diretto No. 2 which only makes a few stops.
Boat excursions	The travel agencies offer a number of all-day excursions by boat to places of interest such as the villas at Brenta. Information is available from travel agencies (see entry) and tourist offices (see Tourist Information).
Gondolas	An exclusive (i.e. expensive) way of visiting one of the islands is to hire a gondola for the trip, but it can happen that the hard-headed gondolier – "time is money" – hitches a lift from a motor boat and the journey is taken at breakneck speed instead of the more romantic pace you had bargained for.

Sightseeing Programme

The following sightseeing programme is designed to help first-time visitors to Venice to get the most out of their stay. Places in **bold** are featured in the A–Z section.

Wedding transport . . .   *. . . and Gondola tour on the Canals*

If you have just one day at your disposal you should start with a boat ride (see Public Transport) down the **Canal Grande**, enabling you to take in some of the finest sights of Venice. **Fondaco dei Turchi, Palazzo Vendramin-Calergi, Palazzo Pesaro, Ca' d'Oro, Fondaco dei Tedeschi, Ponte di Rialto, Palazzo Grimani, Palazzo Corner-Spinelli, Palazzo Rezzonico, Palazzo Grassi** and, finally, the domed Baroque church of **Santa Maria della Salute**.

One day

The trip down the Grand Canal finishes at the Riva degli Schiavoni, where it is but a short step to the **Piazza di San Marco**. Here, in one of the most magnificent squares in the world, you can take a break at one of the many cafés and admire the buildings lining the square which even today still enable you to form a strong impression of the onetime greatness of Venice. Afterwards pay a visit to the nearby **Basilica di San Marco** and the **Palazzo Ducale**, the administrative hub of the former republic and residence of the Doges. A very pleasant way of rounding off a one-day visit is to take a gondola around the city centre; the gondoliers are a mine of interesting information about the historic sights of Venice. Or, if you prefer, you can set out to explore Venice on foot, strolling along the many little streets and crossing the countless bridges, in order to appreciate something of the special atmosphere of this "city of the lagoon", away from the tourist throng.

A one-day tour can only provide superficial impressions but two days will give you the opportunity to explore in more depth. In the morning you could, for instance, visit the **Galleria dell'Accademia**, the **Palazzo Pesaro** and the **Galleria d'Arte Moderna**, and/or the **Ca' d'Oro** with the **Galleria Franchetti**.

Two days

Then it is worth making a short excursion to the island of **San Giorgio Maggiore**. From the campanile of the church of the same name there is a wonderful panorama over the city and the lagoon. If time permits you could continue to the island of **La Giudecca** with the fine church of Il Redentore.

The late afternoon and the evening are ideal for shopping in the **Merceria** and the Frezzeria (see Shopping). Later you could stroll around the historic business quarter by the **Ponte di Rialto**, a fascinating scene in the evening when the Rialto Bridge is wonderfully floodlit.

Three days

A three-day stay in Venice provides an opportunity to visit the Gothic church of **I Friari** with its impressive campanile, and perhaps the **Monumento di Colleoni**, a fine example of the Venetian Renaissance. There should also be time for an excursion to one of the more distant islands in the lagoon. From Fondamenta Nuove a motor launch will take you to **Murano**, famous for its glass-making workshops and its glass museum. Finally, if you have time, you should carry on to **Torcello**, where the cathedral bears witness to the island's former importance.

Student hostels

Casa della Studente Domus Civica,
San Rocco 3082

Foresteria Maschile del Seminario C,
Santa Maria della Salute
Open: June–September

Foresteria Renier Michiel,
San Trovaso 1134
Open: June–September

Foresteria Universitaria di Ca' Foscari,
Dorsoduro 3861

Taxis

Water taxis (taxi) ply along the Grand Canal. They are fitted with taximeters.

Telephone

Telephone offices

The telephone service is not the responsibility of the Post Office in Italy, but of the State Telephone Company SIP (Societa Italiana L'Escercizio Telecomunicazioni). The SIP's own telephone offices, where calls can be made for cash payments, only exist, however, in the large cities.

Public telephones

Direct telephone calls to other countries in the EU can only be made in public call boxes which have the orange telephone receiver symbol. Public call boxes take telephone tokens (gettoni, value: 200 lire) and 100, 200 and 500 lire coins.

Most public call boxes are adapted to take magnetic telephone cards (carta telefonica). These are available for 5,000 and 10,000 lire in bars, newspaper kiosks, tobacconists and at SIP offices. There are also payphones in most bars (easily recognised by the round yellow disc over the entrance). Telephone kiosks are also to be found at all filling stations and certain car parks along the motorways. The magnetic cards needed for many of the telephones are available in motorway restaurants.

To the United Kingdom 00 44
To the United States 001. To Canada 001.

From the United Kingdom 00 39 41
From the United States 011 39 41
From Canada 011 39 41

When making an international call the initial zero of the local dialling code
should be omitted.

The cheap rate for phone calls is from 10pm to 8am and also during the day
at weekends.

Tariff

Theatres

Teatro la Fenice,
Campo San Fantin, San Marco 2549; tel. 5 21 01 61

Teatro Goldoni,
Calle Goldoni, San Marco 4650; tel. 5 20 54 22

Teatro del Ridotto,
Calle Vallaresso, San Marco; tel. 5 22 29 39

Teatro a l'Avogaria,
Campo San Sabastiano, Dorsodura 1617; tel. 5 20 92 70

Teatro Malibran,
San Giovanni Crisostomo, Cannaregio 5870; tel. 5 22 53 39

Time

Italy is on Central European Time (one hour ahead of Greenwich Mean
Time; six hours ahead of New York time).

Summer time (two hours ahead of GMT; seven hours ahead of New York
time) is in force from the beginning of April to the end of September.

Tipping (mancia)

The usual tip in restaurants in 5–10% of the bill. Service is not included in
the bill in Italian cafés and bars so it is usual to tip 12–15%. It is not
customary in Italy to tip room-maids and hairdressers.

Hotels and
restaurants

The usual tip is 2000 lire for each article.

Porters

Tourist Information

The first place to go for information when you are planning a trip to Venice
is the Italian State Tourist Office, ENIT (Ente Nazionale Italiano per il
Turismo).

1 Princes Street, London W1A 8AY; tel. (0171) 408 1254

United Kingdom

Travel Agencies

United States of America	500 North Michigan Avenue, Chicago, IL 60611; tel. (312) 644 0990 1
	630 Fifth Avenue, Suite 1565, New York NY 10111; tel. (212) 245 4822–314
	360 Post Street, Suite 801, San Francisco, CA 94109; tel. (415) 392 6207
Canada	Store 56, Plaza, 1 Place Ville Maria, Montreal, Quebec; tel. (514) 866 7667
In Venice	Azienda di Promozione Turistica di Venezia, Castello 4421; tel. 5 29 87 11
	Uffici Informazioni E.P.T., San Marco Ascensione 71/C; tel. 5 22 63 56
	Lido, Gran Viale 6; tel. 5 26 57 21 Stazione Santa Lucia (rail station); tel. 71 90 78
	Italian Automobile Club (A.C.I.), Fondamenta S. Chiara, Piazzale Roma 518/a; tel. 70 03 00
Disabled access	The city health department issues a free plan of Venice to help disabled visitors.

Travel Agencies (uffici di viaggio)

ACI Tour Veneto
Piazzale Roma 540; tel. 5 20 88 28

American Express
Main office: Salizzada San Moisè, San Marco 1474; tel. 5 20 08 44
Open: Mon.–Sat. 8am–8pm
Branch office: Piazzale Roma (Autorimessa)

C.I.T. (Compagnia Italiana Turismo)
Main office: San Marco 4850 (Procuratie Nuove, near the Campanile);
tel. 5 28 54 80
Branch office: Piazzale Roma

Guetta Travel Office
San Marco 1289; tel. 5 20 87 11
Open: Mon.–Fri. 9am–12.30pm; 3–6.30pm

Ital Travel
Calle dell'Ascensione (at end of the Procuratie Nuove), San Marco, 72/B;
tel. 5 22 91 11

Romatour
Cannaregio 134; tel. 71 54 11

Viaggi Melia
Calle Fiubera, San Marco 939/940; tel. 5 23 71 12

Wagons Lits/Cook
San Marco 289 (near the clock tower); tel. 5 23 98 75

Travel Documents

Passport	British and US citizens only require a passport and this also applies to citizens of Canada, Ireland and many other countries.

If you lose your passport a substitute document can be issued by the British, US, Canadian, etc. consulate. It is a good idea to keep a photocopy of your passport or note down the main particulars (number, date, etc.), so that you can give the necessary details to the police if it is lost.

British, US and other national driving licences are valid in Italy, but must be accompanied by an Italian translation (obtainable free of charge from the AA). Motorists should also take their vehicle registration document.

Driving licences, etc.

It is advisable (though not essential for EU nationals) to have an international insurance certificate ("green card") if you are driving your own car.

Green card

Foreign cars must display the oval nationality plate.

Nationality plate

When to go

The main tourist season in summer brings a great many visitors flocking to Venice, often making it difficult to find accommodation. For this reason, and also bearing the weather in mind, it is better to plan a visit for either late spring/early summer (end of May–end of June) or the autumn (beginning of September–end of October), both times of the year when average air temperatures are above 15°C and average water temperatures are at least 17°C.

Tourism in winter has grown considerably in recent years thanks to the revival of Carnival. Nowadays during the first half of February Venice takes on a different aspect and the city is transformed into something resembling a gigantic masked ball to which visitors are cordially invited.

Apart from these "mad days", a visit in winter has the added advantage of enabling the visitor to see Venice in peace. Nor should it be assumed that the weather at this time will be noticeably cold. The average temperature from December to February is about 6°C, although there is often a spell of bad weather at the start of the New Year.

Youth Hostels (Alberghi della Gioventù)

Ostello Venezia, Albergo della Gioventù
Fondamenta Zitella 86 (Isola della Giudecca);
tel. 5 23 82 11
Open: Feb. 1st–Dec. 15th

See entry

Student hostels

Useful Telephone Numbers at a Glance

Emergency calls (throughout Italy)	113
Ambulance (Pronto Soccorso Autoambulanze – Blue Cross)	
Venice	52 30 00
Mestre	98 89 88
Breakdown assistance	116
Emergency (general: fire, ambulance, police)	113
First Aid: (Croce Rossa – Red Cross)	
Venice	8 63 46
Mestre	95 09 88
Ambulatorio Lido	76 87 00
Information	
Automobile Club Italiano (ACI)	5 20 03 00
Airlines	
Alitalia	5 26 61 11
British Airways	5 28 20 26 (BA)
TWA	5 20 32 19 (TWA)
Airport	66 11 11
Consulate	
Great Britain	5 22 72 07
Hospitals	
Ospedale Civile, Venice	78 45 16
Ospedale Civile, Mestre	95 79 44, 98 12 00
Ospedale al Mare, Lido	76 87 00
Lost property	
Municipal transport	78 03 10
Police	
Questura (Police Headquarters, Passport and Aliens Department)	5 20 32 22
Carabinieri, Venice	112
Carabinieri, Mestre	112
Polizia Stradale (traffic police), Mestre	5 61 11, 96 17 22
Vigili Urbani (municipal police), Venice	5 22 40 63
Vigili Urbani, Mestre	5 05 61 03
Tourist offices	
Azienda Autonoma di Soggiorno e Turismo	5 29 87 11
Uffici Comune Turismo	70 07 92
Uffici Informazioni E.P.T.	5 22 63 56
Uffici Informazioni F.S. (railways)	71 90 78
Telegrams	186
Telephone	
Dialling code for the United Kingdom	00 44
Dialling code for United States and Canada	001
Dialling code for Venice from the United Kingdom	00 39 41
Dialling code for Venice from the United States and Canada	011 39 41

Index

Imprint

88 colour photographs, 1 graphic illustration, 10 plans, 1 coat-of-arms, 1 large city map

Conception: Redaktionbüro Harenberg Schwerte

German text: Dr Madeleine Reincke, Ulrich Ritter

Editorial work and additional material: Baedeker-Redaktion

General Direction: Dr Peter Baumgarten, Baedeker Stuttgart

Cartography: Gart Oberländer, Munich
        Georg Schiffner, Lahr (city map)

Source of Illustrations: Dr Madeleine Reincke (61), dpa (5), Historia-Photo (6), Italian Tourist Office (1), Wilhelm Rogge (5), Hans Rudolf Uthoff (10)

Original English Translation: Babel Translations, Norwich

Additional text: Alec Court, Crispin Warren

Editorial work: Alec Court

5th English edition 1995, revised and extended

© Baedeker Stuttgart
Original German edition 1995

© 1995 Jarrold and Sons Ltd
English language edition worldwide

© 1995 The Automobile Association: United Kingdom and Ireland

Published in the United States by:
Macmillan Travel
A Simon & Schuster Macmillan Company
1633 Broadway
New York, NY 10019–6785

Macmillan is a registered trademark of Macmillan, Inc.

Distributed in the United Kingdom by the Publishing Division of the Automobile Association, Fanum House, Basingstoke, Hampshire RG21 2EA

Licensed user: Mairs Geographischer Verlag GmbH & Co., Ostfildern-Kemnat bei Stuttgart

The name *Baedeker* is a registered trademark

A CIP catalogue record of this book is available from the British Library

Printed in Italy by G. Canale & C.S.p.A – Borgaro T.se –Turin

ISBN 0–02–860085–1 US and Canada
    0 7495 1136 2 UK